Come

Come

The Spiritual Journey
of
Mata Yogananda Mahasaya Dharma

Daoseva Press

Second edition (revised and expanded) © 2003

First impression © 1994

© Self Realization Meditation Healing Centre 2003

1 3 5 7 9 8 6 4 2

The Self Realization Meditation Healing Centre
was founded by Mata Yogananda and Peter Sevananda
and the Daoseva Press is its publishing branch.

ISBN   0 9522734 5 4

British Library Cataloguing–in–Publication Data.
A catalogue record for this book is available from the British Library.

Typesetting in Della Robbia 12/14pt
by Daoseva Press

Printed and bound in Great Britain by
J. H. Haynes & Co. Ltd, Sparkford, UK

My thanks to God and the Masters.

My deep gratitude to all those who have helped towards getting *Come* published.

For typing my difficult writings, proof reading — many times over, and the tireless work towards the project given so freely and lovingly by all concerned.

And to all those with patience who dearly wished to read the book proof, but had to wait patiently until it was published.

This book is dedicated to
Peter Sevananda
my husband,
the Alpha–Omega family,
and my worldwide family
for the love
and devotion that they
have shown me.

This Book
is written to motivate
and help all
to
Self–Realization

Times — Dates — Names

In this book:

I have not given explicit dates or times; in fact data is kept to a minimum, sometimes not being there at all.

The reason for this is that the book is meant to be read with the heart and not so much with the head, certainly not with the intellect.

For if you do, then you will bypass the very essence of what is being written, of the magic that is felt by me as I write these words.

It is left so the reader will be able to read, and see different aspects of themselves, at different times in evaluating the state of their whole being.

I will change in my words as they are needed to be changed, in your eyes and yours only.

SO ONLY LIKE THIS
SHOULD THIS BOOK BE READ

Contents

Illustrations ☾

Foreword

I am a Guru *NOW — YES* — and it was thought by some that this would be the title of this book. I knew it had to be called *Come*, also that the book was to be written to help those people who feel that they will never find peace or happiness in this lifetime, unless they give up all life's pleasures and live a celibate life.

Self–Realization, a near perfect state, can be found and lived, right now. Like all good things, it takes desire and work to get it, but if you have that, then you will be guided to someone with the knowledge to help, just as if you wanted to learn the piano, or singing, somehow you would find a person to teach and guide you. Knowledge is the answer to most problems.

Having travelled this path, up the mountain, I know it well. Come, take up this book and read on, it is the Truth I write. The Truth of the moment of time.

A Sinner can be a Saint,
A Saint can be a Sinner.

Mata Yogananda

Introduction to the First Edition

This is an autobiography of Mata Yogananda Mahasaya Dharma. Most simply call her Mataji — to a very few, she is known as Rena Denton.

This book goes through her complete life, which is full of life's dramas and stresses, but also happiness and spiritual unfoldment. This book is about problems, love, caring, over–caring and fulfilment.

Reading this makes one realise and understand more of life and its mysterious ways, giving hope to all who want spiritual development and progress.

Mata Yogananda was born in 1930 in Knowle, Birmingham, when it was true countryside, and though English by this birth, has always felt a great pull to the East and particularly to India. So it is not surprising that after passing through the fires of life, and on finding her Guru, he was of Indian extraction… hereby lies a true tale.

There is *NO* death,
Only life after life, after life…

Introduction to the Second Edition by Mata Yogananda Mahasaya Dharma

My main purpose for expanding and rewriting Come with Peter Sevananda is not to do a 'travelogue' but rather to write a chain of events including travel, though above all to write of our story, **how intuition works**. *Why* we should listen to it and keep faith as we do so. For, it is a true saying 'ours is but to do ~ not to wonder' on the whole story. It would be too complicated for our minds to see and accept the whole picture, and in fact, would jeopardise ourselves, our decisions - and the outcome, if we could know and see all.

Looking back at a later date it can be seen.

On our journeys and in fact at all times we worked, at any given moment, with this intuition.

Intuition without ego and pride is always right and never will let you down, even though at the time it may seem illogical to *you*, and unreasonable to *others*.

If we open ourselves to true *intuition* we then find that be-cause there is no pride and ego involved, only unconditional love, that this opens our psyche up to accept other dimensions ~ other planes of life. We vibrate (our energy) at a higher level ~ a sound wave that picks up another sound wave and so we hear and see more.

I do not mention dates or times in this book for they are irrelevant to our story. A few names are left out, for the reason that I do not wish to harm or hurt any human being.

So where a story needs to be related I shall do so as briefly as possible, trying only to show the *progressive - spiritual lesson from it.*

1

A Desire Turns into Reality

"A redhead, a girl?" asked my mother of the nurse holding a new born baby. My mother, who had already had two miscarriages, had two lovely sons, but still very much wanted a daughter and here she was, my humble self, born 4th November 1930 early one winter's morning, after a rather laborious labour.

My mother was of French descent, a devout Catholic called Catherine Reine de Belcastel, her father was the Count de Boullier de Belcastel who had a château in the South of France although he lived most of the time in Fontainebleau, near Paris.

He was a man of many talents and my Grandmother adored him. She was not from such a noble background which in those days was considered a sin, and constant pressure was put upon him to have his marriage annulled; he did not, but died at quite an early age. My Grandmother, who had just the one daughter, remarried and had a son called Gérard, who was a constant pain to them in later years.

The De Belcastel family tried several times after my Grandfather's death, to kidnap my mother; they wanted to bring her up themselves, to have her live with them and become a true Belcastel, which they felt was highly unlikely to happen otherwise. Upon these endeavours to kidnap my mother, my Grandmother decided to take her to England, where she would not be found.

So, with her family and Nanny, she arrived in England in 1900. They bought a large house in an area of London which in those days was considered a 'good area' and no more was heard of the Count's family.

Further problems arose however, for my Grandmother loved my mother Catherine very much and this created much jealousy on the part of her second husband, so Catherine was sent off to boarding school for her education. Twice she ran back home; twice she was beaten and sent back, so my mother spent a lot of her time in her early youth unwanted at home or at school where she got up to a lot of pranks. To make matters worse, she had to leave her pet monkey and dog at home, both of whom she loved dearly.

As she grew in age and beauty, so did the jealousy of her stepfather and she was never allowed home for very long. A Finishing School was found for her at Roedean and afterwards a marriage would be arranged accordingly.

By now the family had moved to a suburb called Hampstead and my mother had been introduced to an eligible man in the hope that they would marry. My mother was a good tennis player belonging to the local club. She was well versed in all the arts and could feel comfortable and at home anywhere; but she was not happy. One day as she was walking her dog to the post–box, she saw a young man approaching with his dog. Both dogs took a liking to each other and got caught up with their leads; talk and knowledge that they both belonged to the same tennis club ensued and I believe they fell in love at first sight. Her stepfather, hearing of this developing friendship, decided she should be married straight away and Stanley Stuart, which was this young man's name, was sent away after being told that Catherine did not love him or want his friendship.

So the play of life continued with marriage to a man who was Headmaster of a College in Hampstead; a marriage of convenience, where he drank, abused and caused my Mother to have two miscarriages, mistreated the school children and was taken to court for it. My heartbroken mother spoke to a Priest about this, asking the Father what she should do. The Father replied, "My child, go home, it is your duty to do so." This she did.

The war years had come and gone by now, 1914–1918; it was over. My mother had not heard a word from Stanley though she had not forgotten him. It was usual for Catherine to go for walks whenever she could as this would get her out and free to think about her life. One day on such a walk in deep thought, she heard a voice say, "Hello Catherine", and looking up, she saw Stanley standing there. Their eyes showed the love they had for each other and at a later date, while chaperoned, as was the need for a lady in those days, Stanley showed Catherine a photograph he had kept of her all those years.

Stanley, like a lot of young men, had enlisted when war broke out, had joined the RAF[1], had been shot down, gassed and was invalided out of the RAF. He was now employed as manager of Spaldings, a large sports store in Holborn and still continued playing tennis.

Would she get an annulment on grounds of cruelty and marry him? "Yes, I will, as soon as possible," Catherine said, and meanwhile she would stay with the friend who was chaperoning her to these meetings between them.

This marriage being unacceptable to Catherine's parents, they were both ostracised by the family. Stanley's parents, Mr and Mrs Nicholson, who were of Scottish descent and of Wesleyan religion, welcomed them with open arms and had a great understanding of the situation — which would have been unusual in those days.

Their early married days started humbly in one room in London, with very little money, hardly any furniture and a baby expected. Theirs was a *love* of great depth which endures for all time.

My father, although he was suffering ill health, was asked to take over the Spaldings shop in the City of Birmingham, which he did, but they never felt at home there; although eventually they had a comfortable house in Knowle where my mother had her family, Michael, her first son eldest by nine years, Ian her second son and then her daughter, a year later.

Judy Rena Nicholson was the daughter my mother wanted, to complete her family. By all accounts I was a rather big, long skinny baby with a face sporting a 'turned up nose' and reddish hair. To make up for this I was a happy baby that slept well and gave very little trouble. This state did not last long, for at three years old I became strong-willed, disobedient and fretful and only happy on my own or with my brothers. At that age I would try to dance and fell down repeatedly, until one day my mother decided to send me to the nearest ballet school in Solihull; from then on I was a re-formed character and wanted to dance all the time.

We moved to Solihull soon after this and I was sent to a private girls school in the hope they would make something of me academically, but my heart had already been won by ballet and I now wanted to be a ballerina. The school's head was a woman called Miss Roberts, a stern, but just person who seemed to think I had my merits, though much of my stay was spent in her office with dire warnings of what would become of me if I continued dancing on the desks when the teacher was out of the room.

I was taller than most for my age which was a great problem to me as I found I was being put in a different class because of my height, not my abilities, so the work was always difficult for me, and my interest waned leaving only the sports side to draw me; along with the plays we would put on periodically. My performance as the back of a horse earned me great laughs as my head seemed to like its vertical position more than its lateral one. I decided to improvise the Pied Piper of London 'just a little' and the rats didn't know whether they were coming or going, but it got a laugh and I then realised that though shy at heart, on stage I could be anyone and do anything.

Meanwhile, my brothers brought me up like another brother; taught me the social etiquette of boxing, climbing trees and how to toss their friends over my shoulders, much to mother's horror.

My mother used to allow us many friends and would use her abilities as a *Cordon Bleu* chef to delight our palate. At this time, a change was taking place in our lives. My father was not a well man, he had cancer and mother took him to all the specialists she knew to find a cure. We moved to a smaller house in Acocks Green, Birmingham where my mother took in paying guests, and this is where my education in life really began.

Until this move, apart from the time with my brothers, I had felt a misfit; boys and gossip were not for me. I wanted 'something' — not knowing what or where it was, a great sadness would come upon me which was upsetting for those around me, as they could not help.

Our paying guests were municipal workers who, during the war needed housing, while helping the war effort. We had men from all walks of life and as varied a bunch as ever there was. I would help in the house as much as possible as it was more fun than school and faking sickness was to become a habit; then I would watch, listen and learn. I fell hopelessly in love with a tall dark, good looking man who never knew I existed.

Mother helped many people, a kind man who had had one too many to drink; a married couple who needed counselling; one of the guests who was not happy at work; and many other problems besides these, were sorted out. Mother was a good listener and always ready to help. My father was ill, but I never heard my mother complain. She had put on a lot of weight, by now, but had a beautiful smile and a lovely sense of humour to go with it. From this I learnt many things — one being that all peoples problems are equal and need caring for.

My eldest brother meanwhile, had taken a liking to music and we had many musical evenings in which I would heartily join. The bombing raids had started to be increased by the Germans now, and began falling all around us. Mother wanted to evacuate my younger brother and myself but we would not go and eventually mother gave in, at the same time saying we would be better off in London; little did she know that we would go there and not escape the bombing, but would see another specialist for father. I was highly delighted as I had been promised that if we ever went to London, I would be allowed to train to become a ballerina. I was by this time ten and a half years of age.

For the journey my mother arranged a special train compartment for my father who was suffering greatly by now, and for the rest of the family. No expense was spared, though at that time we did not realise this. We arrived in London to stay with an Auntie Lilley in Euston while mother looked for a house.

After much searching she found a suitable place in Hampstead, North London in Wedderburn Road. We loved the house which had big airy rooms, a solid oak stair bannister, mahogany doors and floors completely in parquet. The garden was large with trees, shrubs and many flowers. Our pantry was as large as a small boxroom and I found great delights for a child's eyes in there.

Having escaped the bombs in Birmingham we had arrived in London just in time for the bombs called the *Doodlebugs*; these would fly unmanned like a plane but rocket propelled and then would suddenly stop and dive to earth. Mother had a Morrison shelter installed in our enormous kitchen/dining room, next to the kitchen proper. We had great fun talking and making a lot of noise when the air raids came at night and we could get up and go downstairs — that was until we decided it wasn't fun any longer and then poor mother had a job to get us out of bed, or stop us from looking out of the window at the dog fights taking place in the sky.

During this time mother had got me accepted by Madame Espinosa of the then International Ballet Company, which has since been incorporated with the Royal Ballet. I was ecstatic with joy and felt life had no better thing to offer me than this. Michael had joined the Air Force and my brother Ian was sent to a local private school for boys. I had a special tutor for my studies and he must have been *special* to put up with me. Father's health was failing; specialists were consulted, but to no avail. Mother heard of a medium near us who was said to help people. In desperation, she went, taking me with her for support. I remember the house was big, dark and smelt musky and the lady spoke words that even at my tender years I knew instinctively were rubbish. When we left my mother was happier — I was not. The medium had said my father would get better. In these circumstances it made it much worse for my mother when father died a few months afterwards, and from then on I was wary of all mediums.

My father was a good man, firm with us but he only used his hand on us when necessary and though in pain, he never complained or spoke to us harshly unless we deserved it. The love between mother and father to the day of their parting was a pleasure to behold. I remember on the day he died, I knelt down with my mother — she told me I should leave the room, but somehow she seemed to need me there. As I knelt I could not understand her complete grief but I prayed and asked that I might experience and know suffering which would help *me* understand and help people: that was the first time it came to me properly. "I want to be able to help people." *Growing up fast.*

Yes, it was a lovely old house we lived in, but the reason my mother was able to purchase it was due to the amount of repair needed, which in turn took most of our savings. This did not deter Mother though, she told us, "Darlings, I shall have to take in paying guests again. We need money to live and also to keep you to a good ballet school". I did not like the idea of the lack of privacy once more, and the work it would entail for us all, but the thought of training in ballet seemed to make things all right. Living in Wedderburn Road, Hampstead was not easy in those days; it was a prosperous area (and still is), and people did *not* take in paying guests, most people had money and good positions in life. Those who did work spent their time socialising, partying and going to the theatre and only Europeans lived there — heaven help anyone with a darker skin. This was soon to change and not being aware of this at the time, I only absorbed the good fruits.

Our house, due to my mother's hospitality and *Cordon Bleu* cooking was soon full to overflowing, with Captains, Majors, Doctors, a Priest from St. Mayo, France and a director of films, to name but a few. One day my mother was told that there were people from abroad in need of accommodation — would she consider taking them, "Yes," she said, "of course I will, they are all human be-ings."

I was now looking older than my twelve years of age and could be taken for fifteen. I therefore decided to try and earn a little money while waiting for my big chance in life. It was not difficult to get a part–time job in a hairdressers nearby where I was fascinated by all that went on. I was soon shampooing, *Marcel Waving* and I helped with the *Eugene Perming* when allowed. I loved listening to the women as they told us of their lives and problems. They found my hands were comforting and took many a headache away. My train-ing meant no wages, but tips were plentiful and thus in a small way, I was able to contribute something towards my keep. I joined the local dramatic society which took all age groups and apart from a few hours spent with a local scholastic tutor, I had time to spend, as I loved doing, with my mother.

Soon, we were able to afford Charlie the gardener, an old man with a cheeky grin, who loved and tended the garden for years. Then there was Gertie who I'm sure was German but she denied it. She was very hard working, slim in build with greying dark hair, piercing eyes and she moved like a ferret, never remaining still for more than one minute.

My love at being with mother increased as she took in overseas people. A Burmese family, whom I got to know well, would invite me in to sit on the floor and have snacks with them (unknown to mother). A Dr. Loke from China who worked in a London hospital, loved opera and used to keep me enraptured with his life and the Arts. Many nationalities stayed; Africans, Indians, Australians and Swedes, they all came and I watched, listened and learnt. At week-ends it became my job to show our visitors the sights of London. These people were of course first scrutinised by my mother. Many an afternoon was spent at the Museums, Galleries and the Tower of London. It was unusual for one so young to be allowed to do these things, but my brothers were unable to, and my mother had complete trust in me and everyone else. I, in turn, in my innocence felt the same but I know that today to be so trusting would be folly, though at heart I still feel the same and prefer to completely trust people until proved wrong. In *true faith* does one very rarely get let down; it is *lack* of it that does.

"Judy, Madame Espinosa of the International Ballet wants to meet you tomorrow and see if you are suitable for her to train you as a ballerina." My heart leapt; at last I would be able to dance — there was no thought of her not taking me. My dream had always been this, to dance, to be a ballerina.

I could not sleep that night with the excitement and the day-light never seemed to come. I remember feeling it had to happen, and it did. Madame Espinosa was a slight, not so young lady with a stern air about her. She watched me dance, asked me to perform certain steps of a ballet, *jetés* and *pliés* and then turning to Mother said, "She will do, if she doesn't grow too much in the meantime". "Was that all?" I thought, "No further words — after — waiting and longing — so long." These thoughts obliterated her last remark from my memory and so a few days later my training with Madame started. No one knows, unless they have ever trained with such a teacher, how vigorous the training is and how little encouragement one gets. It is taken for granted that you work hard and your limbs must go in any direction you want them to. I loved every minute of it including the exactness of the training and would get home elated, happy and completely content with life.

Three years went by; I continued with my part time hairdressing job while helping at home when I could, although my mother would try and stop me working before I left and when I came home. If Gertie was late or did not turn up for breakfasts, I would cook them, serve and wash up until she arrived and not tell mother. Later when I told her about this (when Gertie was no longer with us), she could not believe that I *could* have done it. I do recall that in my mother's eyes my brothers were the ones to be able to do things and that I for some reason, possibly because of my reticence, could not — my fault, not hers I'm sure.

The day came when mother said, "Madame," as she was called, had asked her to come along the next day with me; "it must be you are doing well, darling," she said — but *no* — it turned out I had grown too quickly and would be too tall to be able to perform in the Ballet Company. My work, she informed my mother, was exemplary. I had grace and poise, except for my height I could have been a ballerina but she could no longer train me — would I consider another form of dance? The thought that I could have been a good ballerina if it had not been for my height, once again added to my suffering and the tears came — I could not hold them back.

The following day, my mother, knowing how upset I was, contacted a stage school called *Italia Conti*; a very reputable school who trained girls and boys in tap, ballet, singing, drama and deportment — in fact a full and complete training. I was told a great many theatrical productions drew students from this school for their chorus lines and other parts — would this interest me? As they wanted to interview me as soon as possible and as it was mid–term, of course my answer was, "Yes, when can I go?". My mother said she would telephone and make an appointment the following week not waiting for the next term. They took me and once again my heart sang.

I should mention that when my father died, my mother started taking me to most of the suitable London shows including not only drama and farce, but ballet and opera and sometimes music hall review. We went out to restaurants like the *Comedy of Leicester Square*, the *Savoy* and the *Regent Hotel* tea dances. How I enjoyed these times. I do believe it helped mother over the pain and the loneliness of my father's passing, but also she had been to finishing school and though rather young, she decided it was time I was educated in a proper manner.

I was shown and taught how to tip waiters, read menus and always be polite, but not too familiar. All this information stood me in good stead in years to come. But the facts of life, though holding no interest at that moment of time, never were told to me and my menstruation which began at eleven years was considered something not to talk about and to pretend it was not there except that I should not cycle, climb hills or over–exert myself. My mother, though wonderful and broad–minded in many ways, was precise in others.

My brothers and myself were brought up in the Church of England religion. When father died, my mother returned to the Roman Catholic faith and asked us if we would like to change. My youngest brother Ian, would not, as he felt there was no God as father died. Michael said he would and I, seeing how much she wanted us to, also said yes. So a late confirmation into the faith took place. I had a Sister Edmund take my catechism; her loving saintliness truly inspired me and I thought I had found God at last.

Father Bernard became my Godfather on my confirmation day. He was a truly spiritual soul, gentle and caring, very much like my father was. He would keep a gentle eye on me without making himself felt. The Dominican Priory where he lived, housed many such Priests, one being Father Anthony, as he was known to us. He was a great scholar yet at the same time he was a practical and down to earth person, who for many years helped delinquent and difficult boys.

One time when I was thinking of leaving home and getting engaged to a man fifteen years my senior, he somehow talked me out of doing either of them without my realising he had done so — I was only young then and thought I had made the decision… well yes… but it would not have been the right one without Father Anthony's counselling.

The Roman Catholic church should be wide and expansive with Catholic in its name, which in itself means all embracing. Most religions have a lot in their favour; they also have a lot *out of it*: dogma being one such thing — an inability to go forward whilst maintaining the true values is another, yet within all the different organised bodies there are enough forward thinking individualists to be called spiritual leaders. There are now too many rituals with too much money involved for such religions to prosper as they might. Surely the human race needs guidelines and certainly help, but it must be made known that we are our own judge.

We can become what we wish. The Devil … Hell… is within us and so likewise is Heaven and God… it is our choice what and which we are in *this lifetime*. There is no right and wrong… just the level of evolution of *that person...* their level of knowledge and understanding.

Communion of the spirit taken in any form is beautiful.

In my youth if I could not get to confession or mass, I would suffer for the whole week in my thoughts, till the following Sunday. If I had only known then, that all Priests are human and have their weaknesses to overcome, I would have asked then, how can they forgive us *our sins... they* can bless us, but forgive us *our sins...* never — only God... the Infinite Beloved within us and without us, can do that. If we, but for one moment were a hundred per cent repentant of any sin... we would be forgiven instantaneously. Only we can change ourselves... no one else.

Ji Jesus and many other great sages healed... they did not belong to any church — yet to them all.

We need Self-Realization to set us free.

One evening mother rang the Priory to see how one of the Fathers was, as he had not been well. He sounded very rough, so even though mother was not well and in bed, she put on a long coat over her nightgown, called a Taxi and took a tot of brandy down to the Priory, leaving it at the door with one of the Brothers. He was quite well the next day. I am not too certain what the reaction at the Priory would have been that night.

As for my mother's escapades — we had staying with us an American woman who had had her six year old son taken away from her by her ex-husband — kidnapped. She knew where he was... but, did not know what to do about it. "We are not having that," said my mother, "come on, we will get him back." I remember she hired a car and with Mrs Sneyd went off, arriving back very late that day with her son Michael, whom I recall well as he was put in my charge quite often.

It was a difficult time for the Service men and women on leave, sometimes with not enough time to get home, it was lonely late at night and with no bed to turn into. Well, Mother would come across such people while she was out and home she would bring them.

The very first thing she would do, be it at seven, eight, nine or ten at night, would be to come into my room, turn on the light and say in a very proud voice, "This is my daughter". I would sit up with my curlers in my hair — getting ready for a rehearsal the next day, my eyes just slits, to see a stranger staring at me. It is laughable now, but at the time it wasn't. However, many a letter would arrive from overseas afterwards, from parents thanking mother for her warm hospitality.

My brother Ian had a job with BOAC[2], my eldest brother was still in the RAF and not demobbed yet. I was still at *Italia Conti* and very soon back on the stage, dancing. The auditions I found easy. They would select six to twelve of us, asking us to do some tap routines, recite, do the splits and cartwheels. Had we flown the *Kirby* wires? I am grateful they never asked me to sing, as my ear was not true and certainly not trained at this time. After a perform-ance Ian would quite often collect me from the theatre, which he seemed to enjoy. I was still quite naive and looking back, it must have been difficult for him as he was already quite worldly, even though only a year older than myself. I was fortunate to be looked after by one of the chorus or one of the leads; who could no doubt see my innocence shining through.

In one stage production we had to perform a flying ballet which was very enjoyable. One particular evening, I was informed some-one would take my place, but I was given no explanation for this. Now I knew my performance was acceptable because I had been congratulated on it by the two leading dancers. I felt very rejected but could not do anything about it. *That night* we were bombed and the girls on the wires were badly injured in the spine and neck areas.

We were in our dressing rooms, the flames were all around us. We were flung to what still remained of the floor, but there was no wall left near where I was. I didn't feel panic, though people were screaming and shouting. I knew, within, that we would be rescued and said so to the group with me. I found myself talking to them and allaying their fears; the screaming ceased, and soon the

Fire Brigade put their ladder up to the burning room and got us down. My dress was torn and burnt, but I didn't notice, I only saw that so many of the cast were cut and bleeding. One friend who had taken me under his wing was bleeding badly and didn't recognise me as I spoke to him. I quickly tore a strip from what was left of my dress and bound his leg while we were waiting for an ambulance. We were then taken to a school where beds were made up for us. I felt nothing, only a desire to ease other peoples fear, so I took the job of tea and biscuit girl, till I fell on my bed ready for sleep wondering if Ian or my mother knew whether I was alive. No they didn't. Ian had arrived late and found the building had been hit and was in flames; they could not tell him anything — he must go home and wait till everyone had been accounted for. How he and my mother must have suffered, not knowing the facts or details — just waiting. I believe they heard early next morning and the relief on their faces I will never forget. Mother had not been a well woman since father's death; somehow she could not get over the loss, and cigarettes became her panacea. The look of pain, relief and exhaustion on her face when I was safely home had a profound effect on me.

I cannot say that the fire had no ill effects on me. I had bad dreams and was tearful for a few days afterwards, which I did not understand at the time, for deep inside there was peace, an inner knowledge that all happened for a purpose which was unknown to me then. After resting for a few days I knew I could not put mother through that again. She needed me now and I could still go back to the stage at a later date, when the time was right — but it was never to be…

My mother was finding the house too much for her. Gertie had left to nurse a relation and Charlie could no longer do the garden. My brother Michael was demobbed now, but wanted to be a musician and play percussion in a dance band, he was being taught the drums, bongo, timps etc. by Morris Bureman who was well known for his artistry in this field of music. He eventually got his own band together, Michael Le Roy, and was a success. He would practice in the only room with a piano in it. Now, I was learning the piano and was having singing lessons, so I also needed to use this room. Many arguments ensued between myself and Michael but it ended up with me watching and learning how to play his instruments as well as my own — the piano. My piano playing improved until eventually I was good enough to play for schools and dance classes; but I was too shy to do so. Meanwhile, my voice and ear had to be trained, and even then I would only be good enough, if I was lucky, for operetta, not grand opera, so I stopped both. Michael was right, I would not make a career out of them; he knew me better than I knew myself. Michael went on to play with Edmundo Ross and Sid Phillips and to record with the London Philharmonic Orchestra as well as to have his own band for a while. He still plays now, at the age of seventy, alongside his other job as a representative for a leading wine merchant.

Often if Michael was practising he would, in his persuasive way, ask me to meet friends of his, musicians, at Pond Street bus station, and bring them back for lunch. I did not take kindly to doing this, but I did it. On one such occasion I met his friend Bert Meredith whom I did not take to at first, but he became a good friend of the family. I probably remember Bert so well because I could play the piano while he was there, the music room being my own for a short while.

Both being musicians they had a lot in common. I would listen from outside the room, when they started playing on their different instruments because I was not allowed inside at that time. I became very interested in the 'Toys' as they were known in the music business. These are small instruments that include the likes of Cabasa, Tambourine, Chokola, Castanets, Claves and Maracas. I asked Bert one afternoon if he would teach me how to play them and he did, not to a professional standard, but enough to enjoy myself playing to a record when Michael was out — any percussion instrument held a fascination for me. I wondered if I could ever sing in a dance band.

One day a good friend of my brother's who had a dance band in Birmingham, Mr Headly Ward, came to the house to see Michael. Michael was out at the time, so it left an opening for me to ask Mr Ward if he would hear me sing. He said, "Yes, and if you are good enough I will give you a job." I was thrilled with the idea, but it soon changed when he told me my voice lacked maturity and feeling, and tone was not sufficient on its own. Of course he was right and I was grateful for his honesty. His dance band was well known at that time and I had great respect for him as a musician.

I now helped mother with the cooking, turning out rooms, moving furniture and digging the garden — we would also help out at the local nurses home to earn extra money. I helped mother with the shopping and was the odd job girl. This could have been boring, but mother was always fun to be with and I learnt from her how to make the most difficult or tiring work into light hearted fun, an asset much needed later in my life.

It was all too much — we moved to a smaller house in Muswell Hill taking our one and only pet, a dog called Chota Peg — Indian for 'little thing', who was a rather small mongrel whom we all loved.

Now we had only two paying guests. Mother did the cooking and we had a local girl in to clean the house for us. I joined the local tennis club, became a temporary Brown Owl in the Brownies to help out, and took up photography at the School of Photography at Bolt Court, in Fleet Street. What a wonderful training that was. I built my own darkroom in the cellar and after removing tons of coal, painted it up and started advertising myself as a photographer for weddings and portraits. The work came in and I made sufficient money to contribute to the upkeep of the house.

My biggest profit came from a mistake that was made. I forgot to take enough flash bulbs and a fault suddenly developed in the camera. There I was with the bride and bridegroom, dozens of relations and friends wanting their photographs taken and no bulbs. I prayed — yes, I did — although not on my knees, that would have scared the daylights out of them, but in thought and they must have landed like thunderbolts in the right place, for upon getting home and finding the negatives 'lacked lustre', to say the least, I decided to sepia[3] the prints and this I did and then put them in a beautifully bound album. I presented it to the married couple with a heavy heart because they had asked for black and white glossy prints, and a great silence ensued as they looked at their album with neither pain nor pleasure on their faces. I could take no more of their silence and I presented them with the bill and made my exit. Several days later I received a cheque and letter thanking me for the beautiful photographs and album and would I take their friends' wedding photographs — in sepia please.

Bolt Court, off Fleet Street, was an experience in itself; an old building in every sense of the word. I, at first, amongst other ones, had the job of plugging the arc lights in until I discovered why — an electric shock would be given more often than not — just enough to know it without knocking you out, so I gave the job to the next newcomer, but this time I warned him. We had ex–service men who were called guinea pigs because of their war scars, budding actors (resting), and many young people like myself wishing to make a career out of photography. I had an old 5x4 Sanderman Camera, a lovely heavy camera with an equally heavy tripod, and when we were not doing chemistry work or learning about colour and its intricacies, we would be wandering through London taking shots of buildings, people and events in general.

I got to know Fleet Street well and would visit the places where the journalists would go for a sandwich and a drink. Listening to their accounts and descriptions was fascinating — my mother never knew this as she would have gone prematurely grey! The school, and teaching there, was one of the best, but the fact that my mathematics was hopeless led to my departure from the school with a good reference but with the remark; "I do not know how your photographs were so good when using guesswork most of the time instead of equations."

I went from photographing wax figures in Madame Tussaud's for an American musuem, to joining a well known photographer in Buckingham Gate off Victoria. His name was Lee Israel — he was an American who had stayed over here after the war. He put me in the dark room and would not let me touch any of his equipment which included Graflex, Leica and Rolliflex cameras, or his lights, until I had proved myself. I learnt fast to develop and retouch negatives; to print; to put in pictures things that had not been there previously. One day Lee called me into his office saying "There is nothing you cannot do with prints and negatives now, how about some camera work?" How about it? — I was thrilled and my first question was, "When can I start?" "Right now," was the reply. The Queen was going to be riding down Victoria Street later that day, I was to take the camera, grab myself a place and get some good shots. Oh yes, they were good shots all right, of buildings, tree tops, tops of heads, but no Queen. I had chosen to stand on the pavement, my first mistake, take the Graflex camera, my second one and forgot that everyone would be pushing and fighting to get a better view. On my return I was greeted with much laughter. He had foreseen this, and taken the Rolli' — his photos were superb, as always.

While I was there we took studio shots of Beefeaters, fan dancers, military men and many action shots as well as stills for the theatre. What an education.

While at Muswell Hill, I became very interested in the speakers at Hyde Park. There was a certain Catholic Priest called Father Bede who used to walk all the way from Hampstead to Hyde Park to deliver a speech. He did this each week for a good number of years and had a great many followers.

I would often be found with a friend in Hyde Park listening to the varied speakers, watching the way they handled verbal abuse and 'tomato throwing' which was not the worst thing thrown at them. They would continue and mostly keep going to get their point of issue home to the public at large. The extreme cleverness with which the speaker would retort to the many abuses hurled at him and the witnessing of these remarks led me to a certain hall in Westminster off Victoria Street where they trained such people who got up on platforms, to make an address. We, as the audience, were asked to do everything verbally possible to harass them and stop them speaking. We were not made to speak but were there to try ourselves out on the public and get used to 'rough' reactions. I never spoke personally, as my shyness retarded me in that given situation, but it gave me insight and understanding that was invaluable.

This part of my life was starting to come to an end. The carrying around of all the heavy camera equipment, plus my past years of 'humping' furniture, had taken its toll. My back first ached, then pained me and to make certain that I could not continue any longer I became immobile. A slipped disc was diagnosed in the lumbar region and the treatment in those days was flat on your back for six weeks. I was horrified, but could do nothing. An added burden to mother — and not a very good patient. My mother did not know very much about healing then and certainly as a Roman Catholic would not have allowed it. Anything like that was rubbish in her eyes, so after six weeks I was up wearing a formidable corset, so heavy and cumbersome that I could not even find my waist. Apart from this my body was being restricted and although I tried to go back to work, as the job was being held for me, it proved impossible.

I was sent to a specialist who said that not only was there a slipped disc but some of my lower bones were crumbling. He recommended that I should have an operation, a fusion of the bones. Yes, it could mean immobility in that area, but if I did not have it done, I would end up as a cripple. What a choice — my mother left me to make the decision. It was not difficult — I said, "Mother if I cannot move properly I would rather not live", but I was determined this would not happen — *I would get better*. My mother was deeply upset and thought the decision was very foolish.

About this time Auntie Vi came into my life — a petite grey haired lady who fascinated me with wonderful stories of healings and reincarnation. Mother, because of her fear of the unknown and her religion, tried to keep us apart, but already I felt a deep affection for this unusual woman and I believe it was reciprocated.

"Why don't you take her to a healer?" Auntie Vi said.

"No, that's black magic." said my mother, "I feel she should have had the operation." It was a peculiar conversation that seemed to never end, but when it did Auntie Vi won.

There was a man called Mr Stebbin in Baker Street, a very well known healer — "Could I take her there?" Auntie asked. Permission was granted and off we went by tube to Baker Street. If mother had known what was going to happen she would never have let me go and I still felt reluctant about mediums. We arrived and were shown into an upstairs room by his wife; there was a group of about twelve people whom we were asked to join. Sitting at a table at the top of this group, was a gentle faced elderly man; he smiled at us and then closed his eyes. He then asked us by name if we would put an article on his table. I only had a handkerchief with me but I thought suddenly of the clip from my hair and with some embarrassment got up to put this on the table. He took the clip in his hands and gently stroking the clip with his long fingers, he started telling me in a soft gentle voice, all about the past events of my life. At first I was concerned, then interested and finally 'floored'. How could this man who had never seen me before know all about me. He proceeded to tell me all that I had been told by the specialists about my back condition — the treatment that had been given and how mother had felt. He did not criticise or make any judgement, there was only great concern in his voice. "You should have healing," he said, "This will repair the bone and tissue and in time your back will be strong again — would I have a healing from him before I left?" I turned to Auntie and asked her in a whisper if she had spoken to him about me, "No she had not" and I left in wonderment, after booking an appointment to see him again the following week. My mother gave her consent and let the healing treatments continue. Each week I was very tired after my treatments, but in time my back started to respond and over a few months I was made whole again, thanks to the divine healing power and Mr Stebbin.

Mother now started to accept Auntie Vi who had a much younger husband called Leo. I grew to love her for she was always loving and gentle with words of wisdom when I needed them. Having an interest in everything and everyone, I would bombard her with questions on her beliefs and her knowledge and my voice was always asking, Why, why, why? She always listened and I always came back for more and later on in life she would predict my every need, which I will tell you about later.

Now, having two brothers who had lots of boy friends, I had accepted boys as friends and was made to feel one of them. So it was quite normal for me to have platonic friendships and equally I had a few good girl friends and I had so very many happy times. In fact I seemed to have been born with a happy nature and to be able to turn disadvantages to advantages. I do not claim this as an ability, more an instinct.

On coming home from the tennis club one day, after my full recovery, I found Mother talking to a young man whose sports car I had just seen outside. "Hello darling," Mother said, "I want you to meet Nigel." How he got to know Mother I do not remember, but I do remember that I felt an immediate apprehension that this was someone mother wished me to marry. "Would you like to go for a spin in my car?" he asked. "No thank you, please excuse me." I said and made a hasty retreat. Every time he came, I was out, till one day Mother told me she was not feeling at all well and she did not know how long she would live; she wanted me to go out with Nigel to see if I liked him, as her one wish in life was to see me settled. I did and we became engaged; he took me to the Park Lane Hotel to celebrate, but through all this, something did not seem right. I was young and inexperienced — in love with love and he was much older and set in his ways. I was not set at all and was still full of energy and life. We both realised the mistake in time, but Mother was dying of cancer of the throat and how could I tell her? The lie was unbearable — the truth would have been worse, so although it was tearing me apart, I kept up the pretence.

I bathed and cared for my mother hearing her contentment that I was going to marry a man with money that she heartily approved of and that she could now die in peace. Through all this I learnt how to be a good actress and play my part well, while inside I cried.

My mother asked me to keep her at home. I did until she had a stroke — the Doctor came and insisted she go to hospital. I had to let her go — a promise broken. My fiancé, who I hoped might still be a friend to me, came to see me on my return from the hospital, having heard the news, but he did not come to console me, only to say goodbye.

Now there was no one… my brothers were both married and living a long distance away, and anyway they had their own lives to lead now — I would manage. Visiting the hospital every day became my daily journey. Mother loved blancmanges and I took them *every day*. How she must have started to dislike them, but she never told me — I found out that the nurses were thoroughly enjoying them!

Then late one night the phone call came to say Mother had passed; my rush to the hospital and disbelief; phone calls to my brothers whom I could not contact and my lonely trip home to a sleepless night of tears. At five o'clock in the morning I felt I had to talk to someone — who could I ring? I suddenly thought of a good friend I had not seen for a long time — Bert Meredith. He was a musician and magician, he would be in from work now. My ringing brought him straight over with his magic tricks — two naive people — one needed talking to, the other thinking magic tricks would help. It must have looked very funny or unusual to others eyes, but it was company and I was very grateful.

Life was even busier now. I did the accounts and found out that Mother had always helped people with money but in reality should not have done so as they never paid and we were 'in the red'[4] money–wise so I had to let our home help go and take over the cooking and house myself. The accounts I never could balance properly but I was good at juggling figures without knowing how I did it. Soon all the bills that I knew of, were paid. My one remaining paying guest who had been with us for years, Mrs Fredly who had moved with us from Wedderburn Road, was happy having me look after her — but I was not happy. I was twenty one years old but felt very old.

Suddenly an idea formed in my mind — sell the house; go abroad. I immediately wrote to a Dominican Priory Mother had told me of in France, asking if they knew of anyone who needed an *au pair*[5]. Within days a letter arrived back giving me the address of a family in Toulon and a reference from a Father Toulot who knew us.

I wrote and got the position providing I could get out in three months for a stay of six months. The house did not sell, so I had it auctioned knowing any money from this would have to go to Mrs Fredly who had lent money to Mother in the past. This did not perturb me as my passage to France was being paid for by Madame Gerbourg, and so with no money left, a few shillings only in my pocket, I set out for France. The hardest part in all this was seeing each piece of furniture and china being sold bit by bit, leaving nothing.

In case you are wondering what became of Mrs Fredly, she found a good hotel in Bayswater where she was well looked after.

2

To France

I flew to the South of France, having been told that I would be met at the Airport and taken to Toulon. Although my mother was of French descent, I would never speak French to her and was rather rebellious in this respect, so I came to France with very little French at my disposal. How I wished I had not been so opposed to learning it… There was no one to meet me at the airport so I did the only thing I could, I got a taxi to the address given to me by Madame Gerbourg. Looking back on that episode now, I realise the taxi–driver took me by the longest route before arriving at my destination; the fare was exorbitant. I had no money and the address was a five storey block of flats. Madame Gerbourg lived on the fifth floor, so the taxi driver came up the five flights of stairs allowing me to carry my two large cases, to ensure he was paid. Needless to say Madame Gerbourg was not amused at the large amount to be paid out.

My first encounter with Madame Gerbourg was a very pleasant one. She was a short slim woman, with dark shoulder length hair, deep brown eyes and a firm but full enough mouth. She was an alive person though highly strung, probably due to the fact that her husband was away at war and though writing to him every day received very few letters in return, as I found out later, on getting to know her.

My room was a large one with bay windows which overlooked the main street and square, where many a time I was to hear the

Marseillaise being played. Madame had two children, a daughter called Michelle who was five and a son of three, called Jean Pierre. My most important task was to feed, dress and look after the children. Madame did the cooking and the washing of clothes, but I ironed them. I had one half day a week off and my pocket money was a thousand francs with which I had to buy my soap, toothpaste, food on my half day off and any extras I needed. There was only one difficulty, Madame spoke little English and more often than not it was incorrect and for myself, I had hardly any French to speak of which of course meant that we ended up having conversations of a very interesting nature. French people in the South speak much more quickly than in the North, which made me feel I would never be able to learn the language if I could not hear the words, and when I did — I did not understand them … there seemed no chance for me at all!

During the summer months we would move to Sanary, where they had a very large bungalow set in its own grounds with fig trees and shrubs surrounding it. The sea was a few minutes walk away and the sun came out every day to shine on us. My days were spent in idyllic fashion for a girl my age; walking on the beach, picking figs from the trees and investigating the local amenities. The children, as most, were naughty but nice and now I could speak a little French, I found myself some friends.

Each year in August Madame Gerbourg would pack everything up and head for her Mother–in–Law's Château in Carcassonne. The first time we went Madame only informed me the night before that all the clothes had to be ironed and packed by eight o'clock the next morning. My reaction was one of amazement, but it was done and through this happening many times, I became a dab hand at packing fully and quickly.

The Château was very large, old and very beautiful to my eyes. It was set amid vast woodland with many beautiful trees and abounding with wildlife. Set in the enormous courtyard was a well with two large hollowed out stone structures which housed an antique draining system. It was the only means of washing clothes for the whole family of fifteen plus, their ages ranging from three months to eighty five years of age.

I was not the only *au pair*. Each family had their own Swiss, German, English or French girl and there was quite a rivalry between them as to who had the best girl and why. I am not certain how I rated, particularly as on one of my afternoons off I lost myself while out walking and got back well after everyone had eaten their supper — in fact I was rather pleased about this, as the starter had been quail on toast.

The Château's estate was vast and their trade was timber from the woods; a wine industry was in the throes of being established. Our days passed quickly and I loved every moment spent there, not least the large family meals and tea with all the children which was usually *'Tartine'* — *chocolat avec une tasse du thé.*

The end of September saw our return to Toulon and routine. Six months had passed and I was asked to stay on a month longer — then Madame heard her husband would be returning unexpectedly, she would not need me now and would I be wanting to go home to England or stay in France? My answer was "Stay in France". I put an advertisement in *Le Figaro* to live with a family once again and this found me a place with a Madame Fulchiron at La Seyne by the Coast. The Fulchirons were Pharmacists and had their own shop in the village; they had a flat just outside the village and a baby son aged six months called Olivièr. My duties were the same as before. Monsieur and Madame Fulchiron were what would be called rather 'prim and proper', both stockily built with a stern *visage*. Olivièr was not an attractive baby but how I loved him; he was a big bundle of joy and we enjoyed each other's company. Our walks would take us down leafy lanes with pine trees in abundance. It did not matter that none of the family spoke any English at all, my French by now was passable and Olivièr understood me — he laughed and shrieked with delight when I was tickling him or changing his nappy. When Madame was home she would always rush into the room and ask, "What are you doing to him?" Till one day I asked her why she did this and did she not trust me to take care of

Olivièr? — then a very sad story emerged; she had lost a baby in a 'cot death'. One night she had put him down to sleep on his tummy, tucked him up and gone to bed; next morning she went in and found him dead. I immediately understood and took time to explain to her how much Olivièr meant to me and after that she would come and watch us together and join in the frivolity.

The following Christmas we all went to Cannes for several days — I had never seen so much food served and eaten. It was here I was ordered to eat oysters and grew to like them. It was here I came in contact with the social gambling life style. On our return to La Seyne I began to feel homesick. In my time being an *au pair* I had seen a little of France, learnt to speak French and now what? I had nobody to go home to — the only person who kept in touch with me by letter was Bert Meredith, the family friend from years ago and I'm afraid my letters back were very few and far between.

The Ministry of the Interior in Avignon said I could stay, the Fulchirons wanted me to, but I have not mentioned that Madame's Italian helper gave in her notice and I took on all the washing, cooking and looking after the flat as well as little Olivièr, quite happily for a time. It was not however the reason I was leaving; but it was a point of interest how things can escalate when you let them.

The Fulchirons were not prepared to pay my fare back to England and I had saved very little money, but somehow an inner feeling urged me to go back and get on with my life. A coach ticket took me through Lyon and on to Dijon until we reached Paris. I had so little money on me I wondered at the possibilities of somewhere to stay the night; my boat did not sail till the following morning — this was probably bad organisation on my part... I had yet a lot to learn.

I found a room on the wrong side of Paris, small, not very pleasant, but cheap enough to allow spare money to get my hair cut before boarding the boat if I went without breakfast; which was no hardship. In the Champs–Élysées I could not afford a tip so I was not shown out, but almost thrown out. With my money spent and very happy with my 'urchin' hair cut, I set sail for England.

A New Start in Life

My arrival back onto English soil was in the middle of the morning with overcast skies and it was very cold compared to the past year in the South of France. It had not entered my head to think about the possibilities of getting a job and a roof over my head on my return, only an instinct guided me.

Though I had written to Bert and told him of my decision to return and the date, I said no more except I would ring him when possible. On arrival, after a smooth crossing, I found him there waiting for me as friendly and helpful as he had always been.

He explained to me that my accommodation was solved; he was in a large house where there were enough rooms for me to stay until I had found somewhere to live on a more permanent basis. I love England and its people but one thought has remained over the years, that for people to smile readily here and to be friendly, seems to be taken as an overture. These said attributes, rightly or wrongly, seemed very foreign to me and still do.

I soon fell into the pattern of life and several days after my arrival I found myself a job. It was unusual how the job was found — not knowing what to do or where to look for one, I walked around London going into each store enquiring if they had any vacancies in any of their Departments. "No, they did not — do try again", was the answer given until I turned into the swing doors of D.H. Evans. On looking around the various departments I wondered what their sports department was like and would there be a possibility there. I had only ever sold golf balls for my Father at age nine, that was my vast experience.

A middle-aged, well dressed lady came to ask me if I needed any help. "Yes," I replied, "I would very much like to work here, if you have a vacancy." To my surprise the Manageress, as she was, took me to a small office telling me that as it so happened, one of their staff had to leave, but "What experience have you had? — we only take girls with past experience". Here was my chance, "My father had been Manager of Spaldings in London" I said, "And in

Birmingham where I had helped him in the shop." — I was also a burden to him but kept that to myself. On this statement with no more questions asked, she hired me so I did not have to confess to 'golf ball mania'. At that time it was a large department, as they go, with rails of trousers, tops, swimming costumes and many other items — the buyer kept us well stocked. I enjoyed my work there finding people needed advice that was sincere, with a smile to go with it. I spent time with the customers and they came back. Soon I became top sales girl, but that was not enough for him. They wanted me to spend less time with the customers and take even more money. I refused to do this and ended up by giving in my notice.

Meanwhile, I had found a large room in Constantine Road, Hampstead where I was to board, food was not included but I had the use of a bathroom. I needed a little more furniture in the room and this is where I improvised with covered wooden orange boxes. I had to find out how to improvise with very little of anything, especially food, till I found somewhere else to work. My rent was always paid, but my stomach quite often went empty. Certainly newspapers were more important to me than food at this time as they supplied me with possibilities of work.

One morning, reading through the British Journal of Photography lovingly known as the B.J., I saw an advertisement for a secretary/photographer wanted — this could be interesting and perhaps, for me. I did not hesitate, but believing that the 'personal approach is best', caught the No. 24 bus from Pond Street into London. The entrance to the offices were off the Aldwych in Wellington Street. A dusty old door led into a dusty old office sending out a heavy odour of papers, books and ancient filing cabinets. The fact that I had vowed never to work in an office, particularly this kind, did not deter me. On entering through this door, a voice said, "Take a seat, be with you in a moment". I sat and waited, casting an eye over a huge pile of papers on one of the desks, a very old typewriter and more papers; nothing seemed to be in place. I heard voices speaking and eventually a man's voice saying, "Thank you, I will be in touch", and out of the door came a very efficient looking young lady

followed by an elderly man who apologised for keeping me waiting
— "He was on his own, the others were at lunch and was I after
the job? What was my typing speed and how was my shorthand?
What camera had I?" My head spun — I did not type, shorthand?
— what was that and yes, I had two cameras a Sanderman and a
Rolliflex and had been taught at Bolt Court. I could see he was
impressed at the latter, but not my former replies. "I am sorry;" he
said, "We need someone who can type and do longhand, if not
short." I said, "Please let me try," and added that I would go to
evening classes for both and meanwhile I could read proofs, do
layouts and any photography needed. Yes, I would photograph with
new equipment and try it out and Yes, I could put in order the
backlog of journals and reports on exhibitions. I believe I got the job
because of my sheer determination plus the fact that I would do
anything that was needed of me, but my knees were like jelly and
inwardly I wondered what made me think that I was capable of
holding down a job like this.

I started work the following week with evening classes for typing and shorthand twice a week. My work was varied, I never knew
if I would be proof reading, preparing layouts, or any of the other
work already mentioned, and of course preparing for the many exhibitions that had to be covered. Many a pot plant received my glass
of sherry or wine that we were expected to partake of. I always
looked to see how these plants were affected, but they produced
healthy leaves and good blooms without any outward appearance
of 'swaying'.

My life was an interesting one; there were three of us in the
office and we all worked around one another very well. My spare
time was spent going for long walks over Hampstead Heath, which
is large and expansive with plenty of greenery and trees dotted here
and there as you walk; a favourite place for kite flying and sledging
in the winter snows. My friend, Bert, played percussion with
Edmundo Ross at this time and I would occasionally go to see him
play although I would mostly go to see opera and ballet, queuing for

the gods[6] and always coming away replenished spiritually and mentally "if music be the food of love, play on".

One winter's day I had the flu and was in my room feeling very jaded when my landlady told me there was someone at the door to see me. I asked them to be shown up and on opening the door, found to my horror my immediate boss standing there, with a present of flowers in his hand. He had not visited me there before, and apart from that I had very little in my room for them to eat or drink; a few leaves of tea and a packet of stale biscuits. My afternoon of visitors was not complete — yet another knock, another visitor, Bert, with another bunch of flowers. I shall not forget that afternoon easily, for I sat and they talked and the subjects were varied with me put in the middle of everything. It suddenly dawned on me that they were jealous and trying to get rid of each other — this horrified me because in my eyes they were two good friends and one was my boss. I pleaded tiredness to both of them and retired, very concerned that complications had set in where they were not wanted. A proposal ensued from both the next day but I declined both and unfortunately felt it was time to give in my notice at the B.J.

Being basically of a shy nature and liking my own company I nonetheless had a feeling at times, that I was waiting for something, though what it was I did not know; these feelings left me sometimes feeling very isolated. It was during one of these times that Bert once again asked me to marry him. Yes, I did love him in the only way I knew how — with sincerity, trust and friendship, that he had always given me, demanding nothing from me in return; surely this must be love? My reply to his proposal was, yes; the date would be left to him to decide.

We were married in 1956 in the Catholic Priory, Southampton Road, Hampstead. Father Donald officiated and Lee Israel took our wedding photographs; the reception was held where we were to live after we were married and just close family attended. I was very happy and contented thinking that now I would have someone to look after.

By now, my character was that of determination, a certain pride and a belief in truth and justice. Insecure in my knowledge of who I was and my part in life, and though I loved looking at cathedrals, churches and their architecture, I had already decided God was everywhere, so I very seldom attended Mass or any church services. Though my faith and prayers never left me, I was still trying to work out confession, its reasons, and why I was not allowed to go to another church — so many questions to ask and read about. Something restless was within and yet life kept me too busy to search too deeply. My belief in life and people, with a built-in ability to turn the bad problems into good ones, has always been with me, so with no knowledge of jealousy, bitterness or the cunningness of life, a new chapter in my life started.

3

Married Life

I was twenty five years of age, now Mrs Judy Rena Meredith living with my husband, Bert, in a very nice garden flat in Hampstead. I was happy. Bert was seven years older than myself, a musician, percussionist, who played with such orchestras as the London Philharmonic and Edmundo Ross. He was a recording artist and therefore he was greatly sought after and he would work from early afternoon till late at night. He was a good photographer, an amateur magician and his love of sports cars and vintage models took us to many race meetings and car shows. He was gentle by nature, patient with things he cared for, but not at all good with money.

The first year of our marriage was very exciting, meeting new people in every walk of life, helping bind music sheets for different evening performances and going to the recording studios with the car full of Timps, Bongos and Toys; we also combined our photography and would discuss this endlessly. While all this was happening, a baby was being conceived for the following year.

My mother, though she had always hoped to see a grandchild by one of us, had made it known to me that she thought it would not be easy for me and that being a red head I would bleed a lot which would make delivery painful. I tried not to remember these words, but admit it was difficult, although life was busy for us and the time flew. The following September, a year later, our first baby was born weighing over eight pounds with a mass of dark hair and blue green eyes. I had the baby in hospital and although the delivery was easy, the labour was long. We called our daughter Trudy Maria — she was already a determined, forceful little character and did not seem to need very much sleep.

Following the birth of Trudy, Bert found there was far less demand for the musical side of his work — it was proving to be a difficult time for most musicians. We wondered what was the best thing to do and Bert hit on the idea of making his garage, which was in the Mews near us, into a workshop where he would service and tune cars. This took off in a big way and he had several cars from the racetrack at Brands Hatch, plus more ordinary cars, coming in for service and tuning. This is where I learnt about cars and the working of them; many weekends would find us at one of the race tracks clocking the times of a car and being in the pit to watch the pit stops. The atmosphere was electric and very exhilarating. During this time, my second baby came into being but I no longer concerned myself about the end product. By now, we had orders from abroad for spare parts, valves, gaskets, spark plugs and other small parts. I was more at home now doing the office work and would write letters of reply on my new found 'lump' of a stomach. My other job was to turn the valves on the lathe until they were perfect, to ship abroad. We had a vintage Alvis at that time and Bert taught me how to drive in this beautiful old car — I never went for a driving test, but quite often I would fetch cars for Bert from the other side of London, scoot around Hyde Park, and out again, never giving it a moments thought — until now. It was always double declutch with these cars and I loved trying to get a perfect performance from them.

One day, the car broke down in Knightsbridge and would not start. I saw a policeman and asked him if he would give the car a push — he did and it started — "What a good car you have", is all he said as I drove off; my ability to take everything as it came was very naive, but held me in good stead for accepting and making the most of life.

Christine was born the following year in October 1958. She was a big cuddly baby weighing nine pounds, with no hair, but big brown eyes who slept well, ate well and was always chuckling. We had Bert's brother staying with us now, so life became more family orientated for me. Bert, Geoff, babies and office work were quite sufficient to keep me occupied. Though we were making money, we never seemed to have any and I could never understand where it was going to, except I would see Bert come in with lenses for the camera, or something for the car; it never entered my head he was spending the money we should have had for food.

To help the family budget, I took up cleaning silver for an elderly couple during the daytime, taking the children with me. It seemed strange that they should ask me for references — I had none and told them so, but I believe they could see that with two babies, I would not, and could not run off with their silver.

More money problems came as there was a certain amount of recession in the car business — a few recordings came in for Bert, but not enough to keep us fed and clothed properly. Eventually, I took a 3–6am supervisory cleaning job. I would leave Bert asleep, looking after the children, while I took an early bus[7] into town to an office, where myself along with six other women would be taken by car to a block of offices. My job was then to see that they all had the correct pans, brushes, polish and any other items for the job in hand, and then check the cleaning after it had been finished. It sounded easy, but there were a lot of offices plus the fact that these ladies got up to a lot of 'tricks of the trade'. They were supposed to clean each telephone by unscrewing its mouthpiece and then clean this with a special cloth and disinfectant. They found this time consuming, so they would dust the top of the mouthpiece with this polish and say it had been done. They could not understand why I objected, "Well the last woman who had your job did not mind," they said.

Two weeks into this job, I found out that I was expecting my third baby and giving in my notice, I confined myself to 'odd jobbing' nearer home. The babies were well and happy, but I was concerned, knowing my food intake was poor — not knowing where the money was spent, nor how I could supplement the income, what could I do? My sister–in–law, Gwen, would sometimes come with a basket of food for us, for which I was most grateful, but I felt angry that I should be put in this position. Bert and I argued — I was always unjust and wrong in his eyes, he was always right in any given situation. I believe from this point in my life, I started truly growing up.

Our third daughter was born in December 1959 — a baby of nearly nine pounds with a very long body, ginger hair and hazel eyes. Bert loved them all very much, as I did, but my realisation that under the said circumstances I must not have any more children, made both of us very edgy. We were both Catholics; we did not believe in contraception and very few people would, or could, give me advice on this particular subject — as far as I knew there was no solution.

The flat was too small for us now, we needed more room and fortunately Bert started getting more work from the musical side and we found a larger flat to rent in Willesden. It had three bed-rooms, a very large sitting room, kitchen and sun balcony, which overlooked the park, and the rent was reasonable. We were about to move, when I slipped a disc driving the car; the clutch was caus-ing problems and while pressing hard with my left foot, one day, I found to my horror, I could not move. Children in the back, myself in the front — what to do? Fortunately, we were near our flat and luckily Bert had decided to go to the garage early and found the car with a lot of noise inside it. He managed to get it back home and carried me into bed.

At the time I had had great difficulty walking, even without my back problem. A large bunion on one foot and varicose veins in both legs kept me permanently in pain; now with my back, my one problem was how to look after the children. The Doctor came to my rescue — he said I was anaemic and tired as well as being in pain and he arranged for me to go into hospital to have veins and bunion seen to; this would give my back a rest. The children were to be looked after by a family, for six weeks, if it could be arranged. Though being upset on hearing all this, I knew it was a wise decision and possibly the only one.

The children thoroughly enjoyed their six weeks away; I convalesced near to them and Bert would bring news of them whenever he could. I was soon up, out and ready once again for life to lead the way — the week following my return, we moved, hoping at the same time that this would be a new start for ourselves and the family.

We bought a large family tent and took the children camping. There used to be a very nice campsite at Rickmansworth where there were fields, trees and a lake where one could swim, so the weekends would be spent camping and getting nearer to nature. One of our friends had a 'Go–Kart', and this we found great pleasure in driving — not always successfully, but that was the fun of it.

We tried to build up our photography again — together — but that became too expensive. Soon we realised that all this new activity was not cementing the marriage.

Time passed by, our two elder daughters were now ready to go to a local kindergarten school; Linda the youngest was still at home, but was no trouble and soon she had a playmate. I found a young African boy who needed looking after during the daytime. His parents worked in the Nigerian Embassy and needed someone to look after him from 8.30 am – 5.30 pm. It was not so long ago that people with dark skins were very much frowned upon and the *hostility* that beset me from people when I took the children out for a walk was very upsetting to behold — it did not affect me personally, but I wondered what made these people with white skins feel that they were exceptional; of course ignorance breeds deception, but I could never accept this way of looking at things.

Meanwhile, I learnt to drive again, so that this time I could take my driving test. There was enough money for six lessons and I told this to the man at the Driving School when I ventured in to book my lessons. He said I may have to have more, but another man who was sitting listening said he felt it could be enough and I was later to find out that he was Mr Eric Richardson… he was to be my instructor.

After driving different cars over a period of years, it felt strange to be having lessons, but as most people know, taking a driving test is just not the same as everyday driving. I failed my first test through sheer nerves and my second when my test instructor informed me he had had a row with his wife and was hoping to have the day off; third time lucky, but I could not have done this without unpaid lessons, to keep me up to date, from Eric Richardson, who eventually became a very good friend of the family. Eric, who was from Yorkshire, also enjoyed cars as well as driving — nothing was too much trouble for him and I believe Bert and I owe him a lot.

Bert was now earning a good wage and I was saving my pennies. We decided to look for a house as we had heard it would not be long before the house we were in was going to be sold to a property developer and be pulled down to make way for a block of flats. There was just one problem; we had not got enough money for a deposit on *any* type of house. However, I knew it was time to move on and we eventually found a suitable small three bedroom house in Edgware going cheaply because it needed decorating and a certain amount of repair — but we had not got the required £500 deposit. Against all the odds, but feeling sure we would get the money, we negotiated. Bert thought I was mad — rightly so — until one morning a box of chocolates arrived for me; on opening the box I found £500 in cash with a note simply saying "from a friend". I feel this came from a particular girlfriend of mine in Birmingham but I cannot prove it as it has never been mentioned, but I did, and do, give thanks to this unknown benefactor to this very day.

4

The Good Times

I tried very hard, with Bert, to enjoy our life and give the girls a chance to taste the variations in the styles of life; this included not only camping at Rickmansworth, but in Devon and Cornwall, when possible, and we shared the work with the children. Tina never seemed to take to the camping side of life and would pull a face, when a toddler of five, because she had to get fresh water in a billy can. Trudy and Linda enjoyed every moment of it. Gill, a friend, would lend us her caravan at Brean Down, where I would take the girls, with Captain, our springer spaniel, who we rescued from going into a dogs home.

The young man who was going to send him there could not afford to keep him and was feeding him on nothing but potatoes and bread. I met him one day while doing market research into dog food. The young man had brought the dog to London from his father's estate in the country — he was a hunting dog, who was now getting no exercise and no worthwhile food and he looked in very poor condition.

"Could you not take him back home?" I ventured to ask him. "No," he replied, "My father would never accept a dog back in this condition." He asked me to take him and look after him, "Captain is his name," he said and before I had realized it, he was in the back of my car.

Captain proved to be a lovable dog and he became much loved by us all; his nose was now cold and his coat shining. He was in peak condition.

One day, out of the blue, the young man phoned and asked to see Captain; upon seeing him, he asked if he could take him for a weekend into the country where he would have a wonderful few days. We agreed providing we could have him back by Monday evening. On Monday evening we were to meet him at Hyde Park to fetch Captain home — the girls were so excited waiting for his return, as they missed him.

I will never forget seeing Captain that day — he was in a terrible state; he was dirty and had been in a fight... he looked awful. There was no reason given by this young man for his condition and I told him not to ask again, ever, to take Captain away, because we would not allow it.

Captain never really got over that weekend and his coat never returned to the perfect condition that it had been before, even though I took him to Vets and tried different pills and ointments — he never complained and was happy for quite a few years afterwards. I often wonder what truly took place that fateful weekend.

Before we were married, Bert and I used to sail a dinghy, so we educated the girls to this side of life. We also taught them how to use a simple Brownie camera, how to climb rocks, to read books and listen to all kinds of music — which were our pastimes and hobbies. The times spent with them were the most important — to be able to laugh, play and be with them, to show how much they meant to me and how deep was my love.

As there is duality in life — we must have good and bad times, to appreciate both to their full extent. These, we certainly had, but love reigns supreme and if parents can only give love and understanding, though they may have nothing else to give to their children, the children will have untold wealth... of that I am sure.

A constant question from our daughters was, "Why can't we each have a dog? Trudy has Captain, it is not fair". "We have enough with one dog," I said, "Why can't you all share him?" I thought that by saying this, the matter had been settled, until one day Bert arrived with a toy poodle, given to him for the girls; an adorable small, fluffy dog named Cindy, who Captain sniffed with disdain.

A further time elapsed, and Bert again arrived with yet another poodle, a little larger this time, called Skipper, because one of his back legs was a little shorter than the other and he skipped along — now they each had a dog and were *made* to look after them.

One day the Hoover bag nearly got Cindy, the toy poodle and on another occasion, having found a nice cosy place in a bag and deciding to sleep there, she was nearly put in the rubbish bin! This could not possibly happen to a *proper* sized dog, thought I. I asked that no more animals be presented to us, although, I would have loved to have had a monkey as my mother had done in her lifetime.

I must say the girls looked after their 'charges' very well and it was certainly educational for them. When we moved, we thought of taking the dogs with us, but a lady who lived in the end house, who had lost a poodle, asked for, and had our two... they were treated like royalty. Captain had developed colon trouble and became very ill and suffered greatly; we had to have him put to sleep — Trudy and I, with our arms around each other, wept.

I had conceived and lost a baby. Any woman who has ever had this happen to her knows of the heartache and anguish. It was not long in my womb, but long enough to know that I was carrying a new soul within it. My condition was such that it was inadvisable to have another child, as I had been told by my Doctor, and perhaps, not only was I not meant to have it, but I do feel this little soul must have needed the experience.

I wept, feeling guilty at the time, wondering and pondering on the whys and wherefores. Everyone was so busy, no one knew and I kept this news to myself.

Feeling somehow, it would have been a little baby boy, I named him in my heart 'Little John' and remember him in my heart and prayers — he is very real to me.

Now I have four children.

Unconditional
Love
is
Paramount

5

We Move

*T*HE house we moved to was in Landseer Close, Edgware, a semi–detached, with a small garden front and back. There was a lane leading from the back garden to the main shopping centre and to Burnt Oak Station. In addition, we had a few shops at the top of our road; we were proud of our house. Shops, schools all to hand, *maybe this* was our new start in life.

Bert had got work playing with the Roberto Inglais Orchestra, at a top restaurant in London. Finishing late, he very seldom got up before lunch — then he would have his music to prepare and practice, so we saw very little of each other. Neither did he see much of the children, but I always tried to show them, with words and actions, how much we both loved them. They were growing fast and our marriage was breaking up. Our outings caused problems... so we stopped going out together.

Money was still short, even though he was working, so I took in envelopes to type, getting one pound per thousand, and baby's panties to sew together, or other sewing work which brought in a certain amount of pocket money. I made most of the children's dresses and hats, apart from school uniforms, so I felt we were managing.

Bert still dabbled in cars and as Eric sold cars now, Bert would often call him for help or advice. Eric would baby–sit while we went out to see friends, sometimes, or take the girls out for a ride, if he was not seeing his girlfriend.

So life went on — till one day Bert told me he was no longer working, but had decided to become an agent for artists, and that he was looking for singers he could promote; this was a time–consuming business for him, with little or *no* money coming from it, so I decided to take up Market Research. I had an interview with a Mr Featherstone, who then, with a tape recorder, employed me to research all different kinds of foods and drinks. I was soon interviewing people who had strong viewpoints on greenhouses, politics and many other topics. I would take a team of people in a crew bus around the schools and suburbs, doing research into a wide variety of subjects and edibles — ice cream research was a particular favourite of mine!

This was interesting work which I tried to do mostly when Bert was at home. Sometimes I was a little late returning, but very rarely and if I was late, I had a very good next door neighbour.

6

More Problems

THE house was going to be taken from us, unless the mortgage was paid... we were behind with our payments, and this was the first I knew of it. Would Bert see if the Welfare would help us — "No," he said, "I am never going to ask them for anything". Already, we had had the unpleasant experience of three burly men coming to reclaim Bert's car; I tried to stop them, but to no avail — I did not have the money to get it back for him. Now, it was even worse, the house was at stake. There was only one thing to do — go to the Council, explain the position and take over the finance myself, in my name... *I did.*

They had never heard of such a thing being requested of them before. They could not do this — they did not know how to go about it. I stayed all that morning asking, pleading and reasoning with them. Many different people were brought in to remonstrate with me, until one man eventually said, "There is always a first time for everything — remember, I am putting my trust in you." I remember feeling not only a great sense of relief, but freedom at taking full responsibility for the house.

I was earning a good wage now, and in my own time, so as not to disrupt the household, I discreetly paid all the bills, having opened my own bank account, which I fed well, every week. The children were now able to have new clothes, some proper furniture in their rooms and nutritious food in their stomachs. I was content for the moment.

Meditation
will
Bring you Peace

7

Market Research

MY name was now on most of the 'Gallup Poll' agencies as well as several other large consumer statistic firms, like those of 'Interscan', 'Marplan', and others.

The work was varied, with testing taking place inside and outside, on all foods, ice cream, different wines and beers, as well as on things like machinery and greenhouses and the BBC interviewing, that had to be done at regular intervals, to test the public's taste on their programmes. In depth interviewing was one aspect of this work that I found particularly enjoyable, when it came my way. There were not that many Research Interviewers in those days, and if you were reliable and good at your job, the bonuses were many, with the added attraction of being chosen for the most interesting — but difficult jobs.

I made up my mind to enjoy my work... and I did — my 'yard stick', as in everything, was to get as near perfection in the job, as possible and to try and get through each day without any refusals from people to co–operate. Most of the human population that I met, were very lonely ordinary people. A stage star or two would get upset when I did not recognise them to begin with, and there were dubious moments with 'rich cads', but it was an education in itself, which I am pleased not to have missed.

One day, there was research being done on 'Lager' — how do the public at large like the drink?... with a head on it?... golden?... full taste?... and so on... with men and women being needed on the quota. I went out to find them, on the street, and bring them in for the tasting, but because the weather was poor and it had been raining most of the day, it became very difficult to get our quota; also things had been difficult at home.

I was in the middle of several 'desperate' situations and there seemed no way out of them — but I had to smile and show happiness to these people, not only to complete the work for the day, but also because it was not their fault... my situation. Feeling torn apart and wondering if life was really 'worth living', I wondered how much longer it would go on.

I paused in the doorway for a moment; looking up the street, I noticed a woman hurrying down, crossing quickly over the road and then stopping abruptly by my side.

"Are you Mrs Meredith?" she asked.

"Why yes." I said, trying my best to recognise her.

"You won't know me, but I have a message for you." Oh dear, the children came to mind — what had happened to them; she must have read my thoughts for she continued saying, "Can we talk?"

"Not really, I am working."

"It's very important."

"Well," I said, "If you will come and help with my research on Lager, we can talk."

Smiling at me, she came in and sat down at a small table where I was to interview her. Finishing the interview, she told me she was a Mrs Meredith, from Wales, and she went on to say that she rarely came to London and never to this part... she had heard a real voice telling her to come here, to find me and where I could be found.

The message she was to tell me was that my plight was known of in the heavens and that there was more misery and hard work yet to come, but that I must work through it and not give up, for happiness *will be beyond* that.

To say I was amazed, was to put it mildly. Yet as she spoke my whole being felt uplifted, a dark, heavy cloud dispersed and I knew then that I could... and would, go on.

Before I could say anything worthwhile — she had gone... I quickly went out into the street, which was a long, narrow one, but she was nowhere to be seen.

Surely, *she* could be called a messenger from God... and just in time.

8

Hypnotism

I wanted to learn and to know more about life and death, with all its intricacies — to look at all countries and their different races, religions and faiths of all kinds — Buddhists, Hindus, and Moslems, to name but a few. I also wanted to learn more about the Arts, ballet and all music from opera to jazz; then there was the medical profession and its alternatives, as they are known today.

My thirst for knowledge could not be quenched and so reading, listening and experiencing was a vital and necessary part of life for me.

I decided, one day, to learn Hypnosis, not that I believed in it, or knew anything about it... but did it work? After reading many books... a chance meeting with a Hypnotist made me enquire about the possibilities of being taught in this art.

"Yes," it was possible; "Ring me tomorrow", was this man's reply. This I did and an appointment was made. His charges were reasonable for which I was grateful. A few days later, he rang to cancel... he had to go away — a further appointment was made on his return. This time, I had to cancel — I had a cold.

This procedure went on for some time, with either one or the other of us cancelling. Eventually, we both gave up on each other. I tried making other appointments with other Hypnotists, but always the same happened — cancelled... cancelled... cancelled. The facts were, that a bus, my bus, would be taken out of service; my car would not start and even a taxi did not arrive — coincidence? — you might say so, but I had had enough, at least for the time being.

It was many years later that I found out I had this ability without thinking about it... quite naturally — I could send people to sleep or get them into any state that was needed. They would have unusual experiences in these states... this concerned me as I knew I was touching on something deeper than was needed — but what was it?

It was not until I had done major spiritual surgery in my capacity as a healer, that I realised I needed further help — so I prayed and asked. Chin Sen Lu came with the answer:

"What are you concerned about?" he asked me.

"What am I doing with these patients?" I asked him.

"Nothing abnormal," then he added "Because you are feeling it is abnormal, it is."

"I don't understand."

"You have a natural ability to do whatever is needed of you including *hypnotism*."

"But this should be learnt," I responded.

"Yes, usually, but you have learnt this in a past life, so why learn it again — just do it. It needs no more learning, when it comes naturally to you."

"Is it not dangerous to do this?" I asked him.

"It would be if you try to analyse it and not work with it."

I do not mind admitting... I was 'floored'.

"Has this had anything to do with my inability to get teaching on this subject?"

"Yes, it has. It is not in your path of life to be taught again."

"Did you know that, then?" I asked.

"Of course I did," he retorted, and then went on to say, "Natural abilities can be enhanced and strengthened in two ways — by spiritual advancement, or mortal learning. I want you to learn by the first method in everything that you do from *now* onwards in your life." He finished by saying, "*This* is important to your spiritual progress."

Giving me a lot to think about and much more to digest, there seemed no more to say except, "Thank you."

After assimilation and digestion of all Chin Sen Lu said, it suddenly dawned on me, how privileged I had been to be included in all that had taken place, and all that was needed was *faith*, with common sense and intelligence mixed in.

So our paths, so gently drawn, are shown to us, with choice of mind, but reason included, to enable us to make a good choice.

9

Drifting Apart

WE were drifting apart, slowly but surely now. Bert had found a singer who wanted stardom — she had a good voice, but as I could see... she was too comely and was not built for stardom. I suggested she may not be a star... of course he did not want to listen — why should he, perhaps he thought I was prejudiced. I did not love him now, but did see him as a good man who should never have married.

I felt a father was better than no father for the girls, and on that basis, I decided I would wait till Bert left me, or the children left home — then I would go. However, I vowed to myself never to say a wrong word to the children about their father and this promise I have kept. I also vowed to help him as much as I could; it seemed as though he had become a fourth child — asking me for advice on his work, his problems, any girlfriends that came along and how he could get another car. This all seemed quite natural to me.

The children were now finding their feet — I decided to find mine.

One second
One minute
One day at a time

10

A New Venture

ONE day a friend said to me, "Why don't you take up Remedial Electrolysis?" I said, "What is that?" I had not heard of this and frankly, it did not sound as though it was for me. I mentioned it to Bert, at home, as we could now talk as friends. Bert said "Why not?" "Because I have to pass exams," I said, remembering my driving tests. However, on looking into it, I realised that with study, it could be done.

I enrolled with a Mrs Fisher who lived at Sunbury-on-Thames, for two years. My training involved the knowledge of the whole body; all skin and hair diseases, full knowledge of Electrical and Ray treatments and a modicum of chemistry and physics. My days consisted of getting the girls to school at 8.45am; rush by car to Sunbury, which by driving like Stirling Moss got me there by 9.45am, in time to start study at 10am; then, leaving at 4 pm to get home at 5pm, have dinner and then retire to study 'till 2–3am.

Was it difficult? — yes, but I loved every minute of it. The money saved during my freelance market research years came in very useful now, as my studies took up all my spare time, day and night.

I had to be more frugal with my spending, but as long as our daughters had enough food... and Bert — then I could happily put my full concentration into my studies. It is ironic in a way, to be brought up to eat *Cordon Bleu* a large part of your youth, then to experience forced fasting, because of lack of food... and on to 'fast food' eating, and somewhere in between, all these 'home cooked' foods. My palate was getting so confused with all the necessary, quick changes it had to make, I doubted it would ever be the same again!

One morning, I was sitting having my hair set in my usual hair-dressers, when it came to my ears that in this vast shop, there was space to rent. Thinking this could be an opportunity for me, at least to start with, I asked to speak to the Manager, who put me through to the 'boss'.

I knew that business was very slack for them, in fact it was for most businesses at that time, and knowing that the owner was not well, I had thought that renting space within the very large area of the salon would not only benefit him, but myself as well, so I asked him if there was a possibility of renting space, which would have to be a cubicle with a door, wash basin and room for a couch and a trolley, plus shelves for the faradic, galvanic and other therapy equip-ment. His reply was in the affirmative, asking me when I would be needing it and reminding me that he would have to get it built.

Now, I had not yet passed my exams, so to start a practice immediately was out of the question. I told him I needed it in six weeks time and named the day of starting, which would be the day of my final examinations.

I *had to pass* — and it was as simple, or as difficult as that. Passing would mean security of the house and enough through my earning capacity to give the family, not only everyday living things, but extra comforts as well. — *Failure must not enter my head.*

All was arranged, with a nominal rent to pay. I would be able to have a good sized cubicle, with my nameplate on the door. Their receptionist would make the appointments for me, but I would have to handle the money side as they did not want that responsibility; this seemed very fair, to my way of thinking.

The day came for my exams. I was told the examiner for the practical on that day, was a difficult man to please.

I was petrified... and went very quiet. I knew my friend the nurse, must pass — but me, how could I? Now doubts came rushing in with nothing to stop them.

I passed... I actually passed... with marks higher than most and the ironic thing was that my tutor was more upset that the others had lower marks than me, than she was pleased that I had passed. She was no doubt oblivious to God's laws — I am sure I was helped as they changed the examiner that very day. I then received my diploma.

There was very little time to enjoy a respite, but I gave my thanks to God in prayer.

The next day, I went straight into my practice. The cubicle itself was very well made, with plenty of room, not only to work in, but also to house all the equipment that was mine and feel comfortable at the same time. The room had a basin and telephone, but little else, so I decided to decorate it with a few well chosen pieces of artwork, to make it less clinical, a couch, my equipment and a sign outside... I donned my white coat and I was ready, waiting for my first patient to arrive. My telephone rang — I was in business.

My very first patient's case history was of... Spondylitis. Yes, he had been to the doctor and hospitals, where they had said, nothing could be done. "How did you learn of me? —" I asked, "from a friend who knows you." he replied. Though I did advertise my practice, most patients came from recommendations, with various cases of Acne, Psoriasis, Warts, Rheumatoid Arthritis, Hirsutism, Telangiectasia, to name but a few, and although treatment of an orthodox nature was given, it was the healing power that helped them most and brought them back to me again.

Completely unaware of this, I ventured on with my practice thriving.

Looking back now and knowing how love does heal, I know that I did care for all of them. Therefore, it shows that anyone working, with love in their hearts, *can and will move mountains.* I never could understand why people seemed to find my hands so soothing and would embarrass me at times by preferring my hands to the more orthodox treatment. I was just unaware of what was happening, or how my life was so drastically changing.

I had patients coming from the hairdressers wanting to know what I did — my prices — could I look at a wart, their daughter's acne, or perhaps they just needed a massage or facial; I was grateful that I extended my knowledge to encompass beauty therapy as well as Remedial Electrolysis with physiotherapy training. My days were varied and as I built up, so the hairdressing business dwindled. It was an embarrassing situation, as while I was busy, the staff outside would be sitting around waiting for clients to come in.

Soon, I was asked if I would like to *buy* the premises from them which included a flat above. I was told the staff would stay, if I so wished and that it was a paying proposition. Though knowing this was not strictly true, the idea of expanding was very inviting, as my appointments book was full to overflowing.

"I will think about it," I said. It was a fact that I needed larger premises and if they sold to anyone else, I would have to leave. Knowing I had a lot to learn and a lot of experience to gain, in a short time, I visited clinics, spoke to Doctors and looked at the latest equipment that I might need, while my Practice steadily grew. My hours were ten till five pm., and often later, due to demand.

As my knowledge grew I began updating and getting the new equipment — a new steriliser, more needles, lamps and more sensitive apparatus; I also needed new infra red lights and stands.

My bank balance was growing now as my practice expanded. One day I heard from a colleague, that the leasehold building was definitely going to be put up for sale in the foreseeable future. This was of great interest to me for the idea of expanding had already settled itself in my mind. They would sell and I would like to buy the building, but even with my good bank balance, I could not possibly afford it, so I could not yet give them my answer and so might lose the opportunity to buy.

I approached my Bank Manager, as he seemed the obvious person to go to, and arranged an appointment with him. "Mrs Meredith, you have no collateral," he said. "I have the house in my

name." I reminded him; I also had built the business up from nothing, had a healthy bank balance and was determined that I could
expand and remain in a healthy position. "But, you are a woman,"
he said, "Would your husband be a partner?""No, he would not,"
I replied. "It is not possible for me to help you," he said, "No woman,
that I know of, has ever started up this sort of business on their own,
and made a success of it, and some have been good business women.
Mrs Meredith, forgive me, but you know nothing about finance."
This conversation was jogging my memory — I had heard all this
before, with the house, the same arguments. I struck out for myself
— "I am much more able than you think." I replied and then I opened
my heart to him with the truth, but without emotion. "What is your
religion?" he asked. What an unusual question, I thought, but answered "I have been brought up in the Catholic faith." "And are you
getting a divorce from your husband?" — "No," I said, "I have many
commitments that have to be fulfilled and my marriage is one of
them; another is to keep the children well fed and educated properly and no one will, or can, stop me."

While he looked out of the window, I was pausing for breath
and wondering how this interview was going to end — for that is
what it was. He did not say a word, this scared me... no hope... he
is not taking any notice of me. I thought, when he finally turned his
eyes towards me, that they had changed from a hardness to a gentleness. "You may have your money," he said "But the Bank will
hold the house Deeds, and I am putting my trust in you." Familiar
words — but good ones. "You will not regret it." were my final
words to him and I left content but feeling completely devoid of all
energy.

The next day I contacted the owner, and before long, the lease
of the building was mine. It was in great need of repair and deco-
ration. The roof leaked; yes, I had had it surveyed, but that was not
found; the wiring had to be updated, basins and cubicles built in.
With much red tape to overcome and a lot of hard talking, this took
a few months, but soon I was ready to start work on it. By day I held
my practice, by night, my white coat came off — overalls on — and

I became a DIY[8] 'Murphy'. I could not afford to pay for extra help, but Eric was a great support in coming along, when he could, together with others. Bert kept an eye on the girls and the children all helped, in their own way.

The building I had acquired comprised a ground floor of forty feet by twenty eight feet, with two flats above. One flat the owner had already sold and I had bought the building with this understanding. The second flat had two bedrooms, a lounge and bathroom and this was useful to start with, for the girls, or myself to stay, when working; eventually, it would be for a live–in receptionist, or member of staff. An intercom system had to be installed; the ceiling was far too high, so it was lowered to give a warmer feel to the rooms and to enable me to have a large office in the space above. Then, I had curtains to make, furniture to buy until at last, it was ready. Now I had to find qualified staff which I did by advertising, not only in the newspaper, but by word of mouth. There were not many clinics at that time, in the boroughs of London, that catered for all–round beauty and therapy treatments, so I decided to start such a practice. I knew of the hairdressing techniques, having been an apprentice in my youth, though they would obviously have changed. I knew all the therapy treatments for the face and body, but my heart lay in the healing of the skin diseases and the inner person, so I decided it would be best if I hired just one senior hair consultant and hairdresser to begin with — she would have to be willing to do everything, whilst that side of the business built up. I would employ one beauty therapist, to complement our existing staff and I myself would concentrate on the skin diseases and any other treatments that I felt necessary.

One further requirement would have to be a new receptionist; but as they demanded such high wages, I decided to take a girl who had potential and could be trained. I found it was like the film *My Fair Lady* — I would take a girl who seemed quite unsuitable and did not meet my requirements, yet who was willing, and then train her; that training would produce a near–perfect receptionist. The accounts and bookwork I did myself.

As the weeks passed, the clinic's reputation grew and we had people coming on recommendations, from all over London and the suburbs. More qualified staff were needed — two more with qualifications of D.R.E.[9] another two hairdressers, a shampooist and three more beauty therapists. I would not accept anyone who was not caring, or dedicated to their work. I only wanted the best and would pay good wages for them; we worked as a team, meeting to discuss any problems that arose and as the business expanded, I made certain we all benefited from it.

At this stage our friend Eric suggested he should take over the accounts, as I was having less time for paperwork and we were now dealing in the VAT[10] bracket. It was proving too much for me, so I relinquished this task only too willingly. I remembered one time my hopelessness with the VAT and how kind these people were to me on that occasion, but it could not be chanced again.

I was once told, you cannot run a business like one big family; this I proved wrong by doing it, but there is always a dividing line between employee and employer which it is not advisable to cross — they do not like it. While listening to their problems, talking and laughing with them, the line was always there and though I loved my work and the girls, it was nevertheless a lonely existence, but the job had to be done properly.

Now, I had to balance my home life, with my daughters, who were becoming very independent, and my business life. This was not easy, and all I could do was see that one of us was at home for them, and that there was plenty of food in the larder and as much love and understanding as they wanted from me. Weekends particularly were for them, but they were more often than not inviting friends in, or going out to their friends houses.

The most important task, in my eyes, was to try to keep love and peace in the home, especially at this most difficult time. I did not find it easy, and was always shielding someone from something, but I do believe it worked to a good degree, using the recipe of lots of love and no criticism, unless progressive and needed.

The practice flourished — I now had thirteen people working with me and still I had a waiting list. I had been asked if I could work at St. John's Hospital in the Physiotherapy department, for one day a week; this I did, feeling the need to keep in touch with up–to–date techniques and get some outside stimulation. It was very rewarding and many friends were made there as well as an important job done.

Part of my spare time work also involved taking students for their practical exams in Biology, Hygiene and the techniques of their therapy work. Though enjoying this side of my work, I insisted on a very high standard for them to pass... this did not suit everyone, particularly the tutors, and so I therefore felt it wise to resign.

Business was expanding — without the full realization of how it was, this was a time of 'head down' and get on with it. I would have homosexuals, who needed a listening ear — wives whose husbands were being unfaithful; sons and daughters who had problems with their parents... I never saw anything strange in this, but looking back on it, more time was being spent on counselling than the actual medical treatment being given. Everything seemed so natural to me — I loved my work and the money was coming in to feed and clothe us all.

My next venture, because of the demand, was starting up in cosmetics, first buying well known brands and then putting my knowledge of the ingredients into having my own products made up with simple bottles and jars to hold them — I was not trying to compete with the large cosmetic names, for that would have been financially impossible. People seemed to have faith in the clinic; what it did and sold was all right by them. This side of the business flourished, so much so, it became a 'headache' for me. People were advising me to expand even further — "Start another clinic — why don't you?" they said, "There is a shop in Harrow that would suit you very well." "Thank you," I said. Yes, I did look at it, but somehow it seemed wrong. Anyone can do *anything* they want, if they desire it enough, but I did not put money over health and by now, I was feeling a little tired.

I had learnt the hard way that 'necessity is the mother of invention', knowing that to meet my commitments, I had to succeed by not only being good, but trying to be one of the best and give the best and I went ahead on that basis.

I was now doing what my heart had always wanted to do — help people... in one way or another, but the outcome, I could not know... or even guess at...

11

Looking into Healing

NOW, let me leave the story so far and go to how I came to find out about healing. Having found, and made my way in life, to a certain extent, I now felt able to contact my Auntie Vi who lived in Highgate, Auntie Margery, who lived in Chislehurst, Kent and also my brothers; I loved them, but knew we did not understand each other. They did not want me to marry Bert; they rather disregarded me as a silly girl, and were too busy to find out my worth… whatever that may be. However, acknowledging that time only will mature and soften us to accept each other at our level of evolution, I felt I had to find my feet — and for this reason only — before I could contact them again properly. Although, as I have already stated, my sister–in–law, Gwen, had been of great help from time to time.

My belief in the fact that we ourselves choose the family we wish to be born into, usually for its problems — to help us grow, and not for its securities, helps me see and accept we all have different paths to follow. I and my brothers are completely different and are following different paths, working out only one facet of our many existences.

My youngest brother Ian, who was with BOAC, retired to run a Pub with good food (he is an excellent cook); he and June have two sons. Michael still plays with a dance band and has worked as a representative in the wine business, for many years. Michael and Gwen have one child and are now grandparents. God bless them all.

The person I saw most was my Auntie Vi, an elderly lady with great spirit and vitality, violet eyes and a lovely warm sense of humour. Every time we met, she would say to me, "Go and see Mr Denton at S.A.G.B.¹¹ you are not well". I would disagree, and change the subject.

Auntie believed in homoeopathy, was a vegetarian also and had great insight when it came to people and their needs… this I did not know at that time. One day she said to me, "Will you take me up to S.A.G.B. in Belgrave Square, for a healing?"

I asked, "Why, are you not well?" — her reply was, "I am… but you are not." Stunned into silence… I took her. Arriving by car and parking in the Square, Auntie proceeded to take me up the steps of a very large building, through a revolving door, down a passage to an awaiting lift, which then took us up to the top floor where all healings were conducted.

The waiting room was large and airy, with seats set in rows and the rows were full of people of all shapes and sizes — so varied, they caught my interest and held it while Auntie made arrangements for both of us to receive healing. The next moment a very large humorous faced man and a petite woman appeared at the door of the waiting room and then disappeared with patients. I later learnt they were Mr Albert Denton and his wife, who had been healing for many years. Next a young, pleasant looking man appeared, looked round and then called my name.

"Oh dear, he can't be for me." I said to Auntie, "He is far too young."

"Go on," she said, "He is a busy man, don't keep him waiting." So, I had my first healing, lying down, fully clothed, "Just take your shoes off and let me make you comfortable", he said adjusting the headrest to my liking. He stated that he knew all about me from my Aunt, so we need not talk now and it was obvious that I was exhausted. "You may feel warm or cold," he said, "Your stomach may rumble, but this is all quite normal — close your eyes if you wish to, it will help you to relax. I shall have mine closed while I am giving you healing and my hands will gently touch you, or rise above your whole body giving contact only where it is needed." He had a sooth-ing voice and I remember having no trouble in relaxing and enjoying the comfort I was receiving. The experience was not only most relaxing, but I felt benefit from it straight away.

On leaving, Peter Denton, as he was known, said, "You need to come again." I replied, "Yes, I will." Peter Denton was in charge of the Monday and Thursday clinics, and much sought after as a healer.

Six months were to pass, before I saw and had a healing from him again; his appointment book was always full and if you wanted to see him, you had to make appointments weeks ahead. Knowing this, and only being able to make an appointment a few days ahead, I gave up before even trying.

Meanwhile, at work and at home, I was beginning to feel unu-sually tired; each day seemed as long as two put together. I began to lose weight and my enthusiasm for life. Not knowing what to make of this feeling and when my body would no longer allow me to stand for anything longer than fifteen minutes, I knew Auntie Vi was right… I must go and have another healing. She again mentioned Mr Denton at S.A.G.B., in Belgrave Square — I decided to go and see if he could help me, once more. I had been visiting an Osteo-path, on and off, for a while; he was very good, Mr Ball, a Cana-dian who had his practice off Baker Street. The fact that every time a treatment was given, I had to retire to bed for a day, stopped me continuing even though I knew the time after treatment was very necessary for recuperation I could not *spare the time* — or so I thought.

I rang Auntie Vi the following day and asked her if she would accompany me to see Peter Denton and after my appointment, feel-ing much better, I took myself off to the Doctor's for a tonic. Being a good Doctor, she gave me a thorough examination and found a large growth in one of my breasts; her face showed grave concern, so I allowed her to make a hospital appointment for me, to which I went with a naive concern, expecting some slight treatment. On examination, the Consultant told me I had cancer of the breast and would probably have to have an operation, "Could I come in to-morrow?" Fortunately, I did not realise the seriousness of the case… I had for quite some time now, felt as if I was on another planet, or level, due to the poisons now in my body.

Be
at
Peace

12

Tranquillisers

I was not a great taker of pills for any adverse condition that I had, and my drinking habits, at the most, were a small sherry when out, or a glass of wine on the odd occasion — but all this was to change.

I was getting weaker, as my business grew; colds and sore throats — any germ seemed to 'home in' and have its way. I started taking pills to keep me going, pills to get me back on my feet, tranquillisers to help me sleep and more pills to keep me awake, and a glass or two of something, in between. The pill condition crept up on me, without my realising that it had become a habit. I was working hard now, for several reasons, "yes", I did enjoy it, but as the years passed, it became an escape for my unhappiness, a workaholic… a person who did not see this… and no one to tell me.

The assortment of pills helped me, I thought; I did not realise they were tearing my insides apart and I was becoming addicted to them. One day, at work, feeling ill, my hand went into my handbag for the usual pill… as I did this, I came over so tired… my hand relinquished the unopened bottle — and I fell back onto the couch. My breathing changed; I was awake yet unable to take any part in the proceedings that followed. My breath became slower and slower, my body started moving, gently, rhythmically, stretching first one leg then the other — the spine seemed to be being massaged with gentle swinging movements of my body. I heard a knock on the door, but my speech would not come; then I must have slept, because one of the girls came in to ask if I was feeling ill — it was probably the first time anyone had seen me lying down during the day. I affirmed I was well, but a change had taken place — my body was so charged with energy… it felt alive, as it had not done for a long time.

This was what was needed — what my body needed — not pills. This great revelation shook me to the core and I decided there and then that I would try to recapture what had happened each day, so that my body would get its energy back, without any more pills. I saw now what had been taking place, the trap I had unwittingly fallen into.

That night, all the bottles and pills were thrown away and I said a silent prayer of gratitude for seeing the truth, and asked also that I may be shown more of the truth in the days ahead.

Each day, I allotted myself a quarter of an hour for lunch and three quarters of an hour to lie down for relaxation and replenishment. I thought for quite a long time that I was making this recuperation happen. It was not until much later that I realised that my soul friends had begun their work with me. It was a prelude to the time of my slow, gentle awakening, after an interminable sleep.

13

A Bridge to Cross

had a full Mastectomy performed, as the lymph glands were affected, but I did not know this at the time — "Just taken a sample," they had said when I woke up after the operation and I believed this was all that had happened and did not hear otherwise, until the week of my leaving hospital.

At first when they told me of the Mastectomy, I could not believe it... I was dazed... this was quickly followed by a feeling of helplessness, then anger — why had I not been warned? All the usual womanly feelings swelled up inside me — I would be disfigured for life... would not be able to swim and certainly my chances of any close, permanent relationship in future, must be nil... and what do I do with a one cupped bra?!

So many questions going around in my head. "Can I please see someone, to talk with?" I asked the nurse. "Yes," she said "I will arrange for you to see a counsellor." I had been in hospital before, so I knew something about hospital procedure and its time factor — so I waited... meanwhile, I was getting up and helping with the flowers, tea trolley and shaving elderly ladies, who had beards and could not see to do it. One such elderly lady had a boyfriend coming to see her, and the pleasure of a clean nightdress and a smooth face was a sheer delight to behold... well, that and visits from friends kept me fairly busy.

A surprise visit from Peter Denton, who had heard from Bert about my operation and had come on behalf of himself and his wife,

Joan. "We have a flat at Rottingdean, that is available to us at certain times of the year, would you like to convalesce there if you feel the need, after leaving hospital?" Peter said, "We will be there in a few weeks time — do come with us, if you can." "What a lovely gesture," I said, "Thank you," but I wondered if this break would be possible. This was the start of a true and lasting friendship... but more of this later.

My brother, Michael, came along one day — he was a wine representative for a firm in London, and had business in the area. This was fortunate for me, as I loved seeing him; somehow, whatever happened in my life, with my brothers, I still loved them very dearly.

My counsellor turned up much later, in fact after several days had elapsed, with several nights worrying sleep — she apologised saying she had spoken to everyone except myself... that did not help much. She explained there would be a scar, but it would not be too bad; I would get a prosthesis (a look–alike silicon breast), when the scar healed, and then she asked, "What did my husband feel about the operation?", I explained that I had no husband, as such, any longer, he was not even someone I could talk to easily.

The fact that I was able to support and help the whole family, had resulted in further discord between us. Bert did not want to share anything except all my finances — "It won't work", he told me. I could not live this way and because of the past experiences, I knew this could only be bad for all of us, including Bert himself. This was very sad, but quite often the truth is. We were now separated in every way from each other... but shared a house.

Because we were so incompatible, and I so exhausted, the nurse gave me tranquillisers before he came to see me and kept these visits to a minimum. I attach no blame.

14

A Guinea Pig

THE Doctor came to see me on the day I was leaving; he asked me if I would consider a particular treatment called Chemotherapy? "You would be the first patient in this hospital to receive it, Mrs Meredith."

"You want me as a guinea pig?" I asked.

He smiled, and said, "Yes, but it would help a great many people with cancer in the future if you would accept."

"Yes, Doctor, I will." I said, although I did not believe in drugs and, as such, felt very strongly that there must be other methods of post–operative care.

The chemotherapy treatments made me feel very sick and unable to work for longer than an hour at a time. I was not told about diet, or change of lifestyle — perhaps they did not know about these matters, then.

I did the best I could at home, but nothing prepares you for seeing your own body… after the bandages had been taken off… perhaps my first and only scream came through and out of me at that moment. All I saw was one young shaped breast and an ugly scarred space where the other had been. When my scream had ceased to be heard, I put the bandages back and thought for a long time…

Be
of
Love

15

People

THE clinic was not doing well now, the patients were not coming and my colleagues were losing heart. I was unable to work long enough to take my usual money and they were not making enough to pay the receptionist. I told them I would take reception and try and find out why this situation had come about.

I was saddened by many things that were happening. The patients were genuinely pleased to see me and asked if I was back permanently. "Why?" I asked them, "Because there is something missing, when you are not here." I declined their remarks and made a gentle joke to lighten their thoughts.

Speaking to the other members of the clinic individually, I found that there were arguments ensuing between them; I also found that the books were not being kept up to date, that old towels were being left in the rooms and toilets, in which there was no soap and that all the rooms were dusty.

I then found that money had been taken regularly out of the till, but by whom? and why?… they were all paid and looked after very well — there had been no dissatisfaction before this.

A sad but mildly laughable story followed. Our receptionist had the flat above our clinic, which I had furnished to her wishes even buying her a brand new bed with a firm mattress after she told me she needed a new one, because of her troublesome back. On being told that we could not afford to keep her any longer and that she would have to vacate the flat that went with her job, she remarked that she would be leaving anyway, as her mother was ill and needed her, but her mother only had a spare room without a bed and "Please could she take the bed and mattress with her?" Feeling sorry for the girl, I agreed. What I did not find out until after she had gone... was... the mattress had been regularly fed with our money during the weeks I had been away — what an actress... a lesson had certainly been learnt.

I got the business back on its feet, patients coming back and then I knew I must get away and try to sort out all these happenings... and what could and should be done...

16

Time to Think

*M*Y first thought was, I have nowhere or no one to go to — my second thought was the family and the business. The offer I had been given by Peter and his wife came back to me — a flat in Rottingdean in which to convalesce. Could I do this?... now?... and should I? My thinking was not in the negative, I was just searching for the correct time for everything. Having sorted and solved my first two thoughts, I rang up Peter and Joan, "We are pleased you rang," they said, "We were going to ring you and see if you would like to come to Rottingdean with us, this weekend."

We had arranged that I should drive my car over to their home in Upper Norwood, South East London and from there we would go in their car on to Rottingdean, which lies on the South Coast. My only experience, in the past, with sharing a flat on holiday with people was that it was not to be recommended, so I set off a little apprehensively — three times round the Elephant and Castle... and I was there.

On meeting Joan again, with whom I had only had a brief acquaintance, in the cloakroom at S.A.G.B., I found I took an instant liking to her — in fact to both of them. My welcome was warm and homely without any façade, and the weekend was one of great relaxation and peace, giving me the time to be on my own, to walk, sleep and think without interruption — how wonderful. It was the first time in my life that anyone had offered me a respite from life, if only for a brief period of time. In the past, if anyone offered me a shared holiday, like in Switzerland, or another time, in Cornwall when I was young, they all had conditions attached — unwritten, but in their minds, and because I had none in mine, I did not see them and when imposed upon me, I retreated into my shell for the remaining time of the holidays. How sad, and what a pity that people find it hard to give wholeheartedly. My thoughts were, if ever I have a home of my own, I shall make it a sanctuary for friends and people in need — given with love and *carte blanche*.

I realised, with my thinking, that Bert and I had to be free of each other to be able to grow — each in our own way. Also, that the business must be sold, the house sold — our three daughters, now very grown up and wanting to get flats of their own, were all working, so why not? What should I do?... so much thinking in two days and then back, to put my thoughts into practice, if possible.

⌘

17

Rottingdean

I T was while I was staying by myself at Rottingdean for a week, that I had one of the biggest scares in my life. I was lying down, in a comfortable relaxing chair, eyes closed, listening to the sound that seagulls make, when I felt a gentle, but strong force coming into my body — at first I thought it was my imagination and took no notice, but as the force increased, I felt my legs, my arms and my whole body, being stretched to its limit. I was terrified; what action to take? I did not know what was happening. There was only one thing I could think of doing, I shook myself and called out "No!" very loudly... and slowly my body came back to normality... after a drink of cold water.

I rang up Peter to ask him to please explain to me what was happening. He sounded very perturbed — "Don't do anything," he said, "Don't worry, and if it happens again, do exactly the same as you did before; I will see you soon."

Peter and Joan were expected down the following day — it was near to Christmas, so I cooked a Christmas dinner for them, with all the trimmings and a small present to show my warmth of feeling for them.

The day after, Peter asked me to sit down, while he was there, and see if this force showed itself again. Slowly, my body started feeling as it had before — expanding... stretched. Peter asked me to talk inwardly to this force, asking it to be more gentle and what did it want.

I nearly jumped out of my chair, when on doing this, a voice answered my question.

Peter now asked me to speak out loud, so he could hear what I was saying, I said, "Who are you, what do you want?"

The voice said, he needed to learn the art of communicating through people and that I had been chosen as a good vessel to use, he was sorry if he startled me.

Peter asked me to explain that my body could not take his energy–force so quickly, and would he try to be more gentle and make contact before he entered my body.

Yes, he would, he was sorry, and did not know the finer points of entry.

I asked, "Did some soul not teach you?"

He replied, "I have been told we must learn this together"... and we did.

There were many experiences of this kind, while I stayed at Rottingdean.

One evening, I went for a walk, along the cliff top — it was quite dark and the torch batteries did not last more than half an hour before I was plunged into darkness. I had walked deep in thought, all time forgotten, so on finding myself in darkness, tired and also far enough from home to be concerned, my legs and whole being walked in a daze and the pot holes in the ground became my 'trip points'.

Inwardly, I asked for help and kept on walking — suddenly I found pressure being exerted on my left hand and felt a lightness in my legs; I was helped all the way back. I had neither to look down, left or right. Some soul, with perfect and unfailing judgement, got me back home that night.

Most people will have experienced these things. I tell them only to show how we are helped and guided at times, and quite often we have to have these experiences, for our future work ahead.

18

Beset with Problems

MY chemotherapy was still continuing regularly and with it, my desire to stop.

One day, I had a very strong feeling that I had to tell the Doctor, on arrival at the hospital, that I was not continuing with the treatment; by now, they had other people taking the treatment and some inner sense told me if I did not stop... it would harm me, instead of helping me.

"Doctor, I am not able to continue with the chemotherapy," I said, "But I will keep in touch with you as to how my health is, if you want me to."

"This is a disappointment, Mrs Meredith, are you sure this is what you should do?"

"Yes," I replied, "Thank you, I will be having healing from now on."

"I know nothing of this healing you mention — take care of yourself Mrs Meredith."

This duly said, I walked out of the room.

Meanwhile, my eldest daughter, Trudy, knew of a girlfriend with a flat who needed a flatmate, "Could I go?" she asked me. "Yes, you can, if you really want to," was my reply.

A week later Christine, too, found a friend who needed a flatmate to help pay the rent. "Please can I go too? You know we love you, but we are old enough."

"Of course", I replied.

A few weeks later, my youngest daughter, Linda, not wanting to be left out, asked if she found a friend to share with... would I mind? Bert and myself both felt she was a little young and said so, but she found a friend who wanted to do the same thing and her family said they would buy her a suitable flat... please could they share? I had a long talk with her and then said, "Yes, if we visit each other every week until we feel you are settled and managing". So all was arranged — I believe so all our lives would go forward quickly, for there was still so much to accomplish.

Peter, myself and Joan had become firm friends by now and every other weekend I would stay with them, go shopping with them, go for walks with Joan and on a Sunday evening, they would sit in meditative thought state, sometimes with gentle music playing, or just in quietness, when only the birds could be heard singing in their lovely big garden.

On these occasions, Peter would sometimes start speaking in a different voice, it sounded like a heavily accentuated Chinese voice and he spoke very beautifully, on spiritual matters. I could not believe my ears and thought he was making it up — but then I knew nothing about these matters.

This was known as guide control, whereby a spirit soul *takes* over control of that person, with that person's knowledge and permission, changing the voice or using the body, as it needs to. I was very impressed and questions came flying from my mouth — "How did it happen? — could he stop it?" "Yes," he could if it was necessary. I never stopped asking questions, how patient he was and at the same time I was seeing energy in the form of shooting lights and colours and hearing voices. "Peter, can you explain these to me?" I asked, "What is happening to me?""Rena, you are psychic and developing naturally, do not worry I will explain these things as they happen."

These weekends brought much wonderment to me, and a healing power within my hands, which I was advised not to use yet, at least not intentionally, for now I knew what I had been doing in my practice for all these years.

Peter asked me if I would like him to show me how he healed and would I like to help him with his clinics at S.A.G.B., on a Monday, which was the day my clinic was closed? "Yes," I said, "Can I start straight away?" Although unprepared for my enthusiasm, he said he would find time for me.

Each Monday I would present myself to help and learn about spiritual healing. I was a quick learner and it felt very natural for me to be healing, as though I knew what to do and always had done. Soon, after being tutored by Peter, I was allowed my own cubicle and my own patients.

Now, I was not only healing, but being healed.

My visits to the Osteopath, who I had been going to see periodically for some time, for a bad back that was caused from moving heavy photographic equipment, furniture and a fall from my horse riding days, had ceased, as did the chemotherapy. I put my complete faith and trust into the healing power, and as the weeks passed, my back got stronger... so much so that I put my surgical corset away for good.

The life force was feeding me, and I was being made whole. The only injury that was to remain, would be my neck, to a lesser degree, as my troubles and stress were to get much worse, before getting better.

Criticise
to be
Criticised

19

Unfinished Business

$\mathcal{A}$LTHOUGH I had been having healings from Peter periodically, after a six month interval of not seeing him, my lifestyle had not changed, in fact, it had got worse — that was why I had to have a Mastectomy, my fault, not the healing power. Our daughters now no longer lived at home, Bert was becoming increasingly difficult to live with and the business had declined so much that it was now 'in the red'.

I rang Michael and asked him if he could come over; I felt strange unto death, my strength was leaving me and everything was very distant. This was the first time that I can remember ringing Michael for help; he came quickly and took me home to Gwen, who fed and looked after me till I was stronger. They advised me not to go back home, but I knew I must; I was feeling like a boxer who had retreated to his corner seat for a few moments, but knew that he had to go into the ring again as there were a few more rounds to go yet.

My thanks given to them, I returned home.

One day, after a bitter argument with Bert about the house and finances, I felt ill, totally exhausted — I must splash my face and try to think clearly. What was there to live for? I had no one to love me, or talk to; the business had collapsed, owing to my health; the children were gone, leading their own lives and I could not sell the house because Bert would not leave, even if a flat was found for him — a council flat was beneath him. Would taking my own life solve all these problems? I was alone in the house… why not?

I was not feeling sorry for myself, or morbid, just feeling very calm and realistic. Upon pondering on these thoughts, I found I could not move, my body was completely paralysed, only my mind was working and I remembered the last time this happened was when Bert went to strike me and I froze, unable to defend myself.

Bert was upset — fortunately at that very moment, Peter arrived with some accounts for me. He picked me up and on lying me down, gave me a healing. Bert was bewildered and I heard crying. Peter's voice was soothing and I could hear them talking — I wanted to say something, but could not speak, or move. I realised what it must be like for people permanently like this — was I going to be such a person?

These feelings came flooding back and suddenly I realised they had been, and were now being, safety 'stops' for me and that I was being helped to see all this through; as soon as I had this thought, I found my body could move again.

I knew now that my job was to completely finish and tie up each loose end, leaving everything in the best way I could. This was easier said than done and to make matters worse, Peter had found out he loved me and I had begun to love him.

It was not the right time, but we are not in charge of life, *only* ourselves.

Peter had been sports master at Eaton House School, off Sloane Square, when I had first met him and his healing work was being done at S.A.G.B., and at home. He loved his work, it was his whole life, but he found being a sport's master very tiring. After my Mastectomy, and seeing my need for help, he asked me, "Is there anything I can do for you Rena, to help lighten the load?" Now the day had come when Eric was finding it difficult to do the clinic's accounts, as well as his own, so my reply to Peter was, "Yes, the accounts, but I would insist on paying you the wage you have been given as sport's master". Peter did not wish to take my money — "It's business, Peter," I said "I could not accept your help otherwise." It was only a small amount of money, but at that time, it was a lot for me to find but enough for Peter to be able to give up his position as sports master.

For two days a week, Peter would do the accounts and would more often than not help with other important work.

Joan was happy with this arrangement, as long as he did not lose money by it; this help was invaluable.

20

A Chapter Finishes

*T*HE business must be sold," I said to my colleagues one day, "and as soon as possible. I have to give you all notice, well in advance, but please do not tell the patients for a while." They all agreed and found other posts within a matter of a few weeks; I was pleased for them, but the premises had not been sold and there was very little money coming in.

I sold most of the major equipment, while waiting for a sale. Somehow, the patients had, before I deemed it wise to tell them, heard of my intention and very naturally, in the human way, most of them wished to leave the 'sinking ship'. I had cared, loved and helped to look after them and they, in their turn, had been very loyal; it was akin, for me, to losing a family of friends and loved ones and this was one of the most difficult things to do. I understood, and tried to find other practitioners for them who I knew would not only give them good service, but care for then. Bit by bit, as the clinic was built up, so now... it was going. It was not a clean break, but a very slow, painful one to me, at the time.

How many wounds can any one person receive at one time without feeling that they are dying a little inside?

The human being is truly wondrous in its ability to continue.

On Peter's recommendation, I had given the sale of the building over to Ray, a long standing friend of his. Ray then advertised the property and it was not long before he had an enquiry from a man who showed interest. As negotiations took place, there was a clash of personalities and I believe things became very difficult. Ray suggested, as he was not able to get any further with this man, that I should see him.

The man turned out to be someone I knew but had not seen since the car racing days; he was called Ron, a clever person who had built a monoplane in the front room of his first floor flat. Bert and myself would often go with the girls to watch him build it; it flew well too.

I remember he had a suave manner, was tall, well spoken and had a way of taking things for granted and would turn up with his girlfriend at any time of the day or night, expecting food and outstaying his welcome. Bert did not see my exhaustion and would not think of ever saying "no" to them.

So, here he was again — I soon forgot about the old bad times, when he arrived, because my desire to sell, and his interest to buy, soon became the most important issue.

"Why are you selling?" he asked

"My health will not allow me to keep the business going and because of this I need to sell the premises." I replied.

We arranged to meet again the following day, when Peter would be there. I felt I needed moral support and someone to see that all was in order. "Do come and have lunch with me." Ron said, "I have the car outside and have not eaten yet." I knew what it was like to feel hungry, so I accepted. A lovely old white Citröen stood outside — Peter and I got in the car and went like 'lambs to the slaughter', which is what it turned out to be.

We talked over lunch, Ron had brought a friend with him, his partner; they had a beauty business in Finchley Road and wanted to expand their business to Kenton. As we talked, I told them, honestly, how much I needed to clear myself of all debts, how the debts had come about, but how I thought that the position of the premises for that sort of business would be very good, as the community was mainly Jewish and spent a lot of money on themselves. I gave Ron the asking price, and he said it sounded reasonable and he would ring me the following day.

What happened next was very interesting. Ron rang the following day, "Sorry Rena, it is too much money, can you halve it?"

"No, that would be impossible," I said, "Over lunch you both said that it was a reasonable price, why change your mind now?"

"Let's leave it and I'll get back to you soon; will you give me first offer, is there anyone else wanting it?"

"No," I replied, "Not yet."

By now, I had an irate bank manager demanding that my overdraft be cleared, as well as my solicitor, accountant and numerous business people requesting settlement of their bills. Go into liquidation, a business associate said; "What does that entail?" I asked.

"Being a company, this would mean they would take all your assets back, except the house."

"What would happen to my debts — to the people that trusted me to pay them?"

"Of course, they would not get their money, but you would be better off," he replied, "It's done a lot in business, you know."

I was horrified, he was suggesting I let down all the people, including the Bank Manager, when they had all trusted me — I could not do it; my self-respect would not let me be. Being grateful for his interest, I said "Thank you", but that I would not be content until I had paid back everything. His eyes showed lack of respect for my decision and how stupid he thought I was being.

It did not matter.

What transpired was, I realised, a psychological 'browbeating', by Ron, who was slowly but surely 'wearing me down', until I was feeling on the verge of a breakdown. No one had approached me to buy the building — liquidation was out...

I sold it to him, with as little fuss as possible, throwing in a generator because he said he would not buy the premises otherwise. Even after this, he would ring and try to make further demands. Eventually, I had to put the phone down on him to save any vestige of my own sanity.

Later, I learnt that Ron had married a customer of his girlfriend's shop, for money, then divorced her to marry his previous girlfriend, who had more money.

A truly cunning, convincing cad — I was learning.

Honesty is always the best policy
For small untruths become
big ones

21

The House Goes

MY problems at home had not eased up and I was now trying to sell the house, hoping that Bert would start looking for a flat or somewhere of his own; I had nowhere to go myself, but this did not seem to concern me at the time.

There were 'phone calls I did not receive, and could not receive, if out, so how could people see the house? I planned a time with the Estate Agent for receiving them and told him the problem; he was apprehensive, but I assured him it would be all right.

I prayed for us both, for in my heart I knew what I still had to do… and that from this decision and sale, everything would depend.

In faith I went.

The Seagull

There were not many chances to convalesce if I was ill, in fact illness was a luxury that could not be afforded. Come 'rain or shine' in my married life, I never missed a days work till after my mastectomy operation, or when having children.

The days spent at Rottingdean and also at Westgate, were never to be forgotten.

At Westgate, I had a few days to myself and one morning, when I was standing, watching the waves splash and foam against the rock, a large seagull came and settled about two feet away from me — he was making the usual noises and I thought he must be looking for food, but no… he walked nearer and nearer till he stood looking into my face, just a few inches away from it, he then danced around making an unusual noise in his throat. He would not leave me and was certainly trying to cheer me up… he succeeded and when I inwardly said, "Thank you, I must go now", he flew away although I did not move, circling me twice before he left, like a biplane, dipping his wings in recognition.

This has never happened before, or since that day with a seagull.

22

A New Chapter

AT Joan's request, and as it was also my wish, we met, with Peter to talk as adults, about our lives. Peter had been married once before, when he was twenty five years of age, to a girl called Irene, who worked in the same office as himself. They were very much in love with each other, yet for spiritual reasons, the marriage was never consummated; this was not an issue, and to them seemed quite natural and they remained in love till Irene's passing.

After twelve years of a happy marriage, Irene's life on this earth's plane came to an end; she had leukaemia and cancer of the stomach. Peter was distraught and eventually went back to live with his parents in Uckfield, Sussex. Irene had been ignorant of healing and therefore *feared* the unknown. Though allowing Peter's father to minister to her from time to time, and even though she felt relief, her belief in it was minimal. Peter would give her healing, if she would let him, but other than this, healing was temporarily out of his life.

On Irene's passing, Peter had the choice of going into business, or doing healing work; he chose the latter and his days at S.A.G.B. began a few months after. This is where Peter met Joan, she was on the reception desk and they would converse. She, being very attractive, with wavy, blonde hair and blue eyes, caught Peter's attention. Joan also had a gentle, caring nature, with the spirituality that Peter so needed at that time of his life, and the age difference of ten years mattered not to either of them. They both had something to offer each other, and on this basis they formed the beginning of their relationship.

Joan started having a healing treatment from Peter once a week and their friendship blossomed; Peter was lonely, Joan unmarried. They met and married within eighteen months. They lived with Peter's parents until they found a flat of their own.

They had a fairly contented life, but Peter felt frustrated, knowing a Centre would be his one day but did not know how this would be possible with such a low income, even though Joan worked as well as Peter.

The marriage between Joan and Peter was, once again, not consummated; I now know that this was spiritually meant because Peter was not meant to have children in this lifetime.

Now, Joan, Peter and myself were talking about life, our needs, and what was the best thing to do spiritually — I loved Joan as a sister, and still do.

I said, "I will go away rather than split up a marriage," even though my feelings for Peter were strong.

"No," said Joan, "that will not solve anything, let's talk some more."

Peter said, "The die has been cast, and although the marriage has been a good one, of friendship and helping each other, it has not been more." Joan said she agreed and she knew that we were meant for each other. To me it was inevitable we should meet, but spiritually, how can this be...? If two people travel together and then part, it can only be for two reasons; firstly to experience and help each other through a space of time and then go their own ways and secondly, if one partner wants to go further ahead spiritually than the other, then their paths will divide. If we get married during one of these times and we do not see it as one act of our lives, but as a complete production, then it is possible that a mortal marriage, and not a lifelong spiritual one will take place.

I believe the break–up of this marriage was the second reason, and was meant to happen.

We both needed company and a helping hand, until it was ordained that we should meet at the right time… and correct place. I had to have my desire, as I asked when a child, to experience all pain in my life, so was it not a good experience with Bert? Do I not have a lot to thank him for — and many others? Life had not all been terrible; Bert and I had had our moments of happiness and many with our daughters. I only remember the good times now. I have had to make a great effort to remember, bringing out from my computer – head, all the other times that I needed to recall for this book, in order to show how each person's path is mapped to a higher degree.

If we but follow it,
Without knowing *WHY*
We will not leave the pathway
and will reach our goal.

If Peter and myself had met any earlier in our lives, we would not have noticed each other… it was not the time.

To illustrate this — one day I was walking in London when I saw my Guru walking past me, only to disappear. Something drew my attention.

"I know this person," I said to myself .. but he was gone. I was not ready for him yet. My lotus petals[12] were not open enough to perceive him and who he was… *it was not the right time.*

Joan understood the situation and knew in her heart, as we did, that it was right. I knew it must be difficult for her; she wished to know what the future would hold for her — could she manage on her own? It was agreed that Joan would stay in the flat that she had, with all the furniture and possessions, except those she did not want; Peter and myself could have these if we wished.

Still seeing patients at S.A.G.B., we would ponder on how we could live and where we would go, as when my house and clinic were sold, the money that I would receive would only be enough to clear any back debts and accumulation of further debts, since my operation and inability to earn money.

At the time, we had a patient, a friend of Peter's, called David who said to us one day, "Have you thought of moving to the country?"

"Well, we were thinking of searching somewhere in the Sussex area."

"There's a flat going in Castle Cary," he said.

"I do not want to move to Ireland", I retorted.

He laughed and said, "I mean Castle Cary, Somerset."

I had only been through Somerset on my way to Cornwall, on the occasional holiday... I could not remember it.

Peter responded quickly, asking if we could go and see it — "How much is it?"

"About ten pounds a week, I believe." he said, "Tell you what, I will go and ring them up, as I know them quite well, and arrange a time for you to go and see it."

We went down to Somerset that coming weekend. It was a lovely sunny day and we needed a day out; we looked on the outing as only that — of course we were interested, but where, and what could you get in accommodation for ten pounds these days... the mind boggled. I said it was too far from my daughters, the house, the clinic and S.A.G.B. , Peter agreed and we continued in silence, with our own thoughts, till we arrived at our destination, Castle Cary, a lovely one–time market town, with a bustle of people and locals with friendly faces.

We turned off into a large courtyard, a very large building stood before us; this was Ansford Inn, where we were to meet Mrs Hiscock and her daughter, Susan, who owned what used to be an old coaching Inn. We were shown around the flat, which was situated on the first floor. It had two good–sized bedrooms, a very large sitting room, bathroom and the largest kitchen I had ever seen in any building, other than in a mansion. There were doors leading on to a landing, that was round, so you would walk out of one door, around the landing to another one. The building dated back to the 16th century and in those days it was used to change horses and allow passengers to rest before going on to London. Parson Woodforde, whose *Chronicles* are well known, would spend evenings at the Inn. His Vicarage was only a short distance down the road.

We liked the flat and the owners, very much; we asked if we could have an hour to think over our plans. "Yes," Susan said, "Please do."

"We will be back in an hour." Peter replied and on saying this, we took our leave.

After touring the town, we found a suitable spot to park the car and started to question the *viability* of the home situation.

"Too far from the girls." I said.

"You need to be." replied Peter.

"What about getting to London for our healing work?" I asked.

"There is a railway station here you know!"

"Yes, but I have to sell the house, and what about the clinic?" I said, feeling a little perturbed.

"Listen," Peter said, "Do you like the flat?"

"Yes, very much," I replied.

"Have I answered all your questions positively?"

"Yes", I said.

"Well, let's take it then." Peter said, and having found all my negative questions squashed, I said, "Yes, let's do that."

We returned to pay our deposit, had a further look at the flat, and did some measuring for curtains; we bought the carpets that were already installed. Then, we set off back to London feeling excited at the prospect of soon being together in our own home.

During our talks together with Joan, I found I would be used in a trance state; a different voice (Aranti, whom I knew in Grecian times at the Temples, in a past life) would come, changing my face, moving my body and speaking in a gentle voice to Joan.

I allowed, and was so grateful for this, as Joan could then feel secure to ask questions about herself and the situation between the three of us.

"Yes, you will be happy." said Aranti.

"Will I have companionship?" Joan asked.

"Oh, yes, you will, and a comfortable flat — you could be near to Peter and Rena, if the basis of the friendship was as it should be," Aranti said, "For when circumstances come about, all profit from it, there is no actual loss."

The three of us had many quiet times like this together, searching for and finding out the true reasons behind the happenings. This was a most difficult and telling time for all of us, and yet wonderfully progressive.

Peter's father, who had passed several years back, would occasionally come through Peter or myself and provide facts to prove that it was truly he who was speaking. I was learning that I could be a good trance medium, how to control and be in charge at the same time as being controlled; an outstanding partnership, which neither of us took advantage of.

In life, everything is 'give and take', and so we teach and learn… learn and teach.

If we do not look and try to make these things happen ourselves, but simply *let* them, when there is a need for the traumas and a right time for them, then all is well. For some, it could seem 'exciting and heady', with the wish to communicate and let the trance work happen whenever possible; this is dangerous to one's health, for we are dealing here with a different plane of being which requires a different type of energy than that used by us. Many mediums become unhealthy through not being in control of themselves and at all times being in charge.

"Seek first the Spiritual, then all else shall be added unto you". This is a true statement — that through life's experiences I have found to be the most perfect way of progressing. These are not religious sentiments but facts of life.

While waiting for the house to sell, I was contemplating how Peter and myself would live without any money, when I received a letter from a Solicitor, telling me that my Aunt Marjorie Nicholson had passed and in her will, she had bestowed on me two thousand pounds. Occasionally, when the children were younger, I had visited my Aunt and Uncle Laurie; but as they were such bundles of energy, the children were very tiring for them, so my visits were very rare, but once or twice Peter would take me to see them, when we would give them healing and tell them of our plans.

Uncle Laurie was very much like my father, very sensitive and gentle... he passed, followed by Aunt a few years later.

On hearing this news, my thoughts were with my Aunt, but later it dawned on me that she must have left me this money to help us to start our new life. Now, we had time to think — a little breathing space — time to build a Centre.

My Gratitude is Eternal.

Shortly before my move to Somerset and in the throes of packing cases and boxes for removal, there was a phone call from Eric. He had rung to wish us every happiness and to tell me that he, also, was getting married to a girlfriend he had known for some time; they were moving to Yorkshire. I was thrilled for him — he had such a big heart and was willing to help anyone at any time without thought for himself, he really did deserve to be happy. I told him this, and thanking him once more for his friendship and help, we both put the phone down.

Love all
As you love

23

On the Move

AT last, the house had been sold, cheaply, to a decorator who wished to completely modernise it. Bert, meanwhile, had found a flat in Hendon, very near to where Linda was living and he would be moving out very shortly... I very much wanted our parting to be amicable, for our daughters' sakes as well as our own and I had not gone this far to even think about letting anger or bitterness set in. I knew that Bert would grow, as I would, from this parting, that he would find peace and happiness of his own, with three lovely daughters to see and go out with. With this in mind, I had to give him time to see the truth of *everything*.

The day of the move came with three buildings to collect furniture from. Bert was moving on the same day as we were loading up ourselves, which did not help our dispositions towards each other. We decided we would have to move the clinic furniture, couches, and 'such like', in one trip and the house plus odd furniture from Joan, as a second trip. We had hired a 'Drive it Yourself' van, a large twenty–four hundredweight vehicle.

We emptied the clinic and took those things down to Ansford, Castle Cary. The following day, on our return, Peter helped Bert pack what he wanted and then we removed the remainder of the furniture and cleaned the house. Too exhausted to go back that evening, we slept on the floor so as to make an early start.

In our dusty clothes, we must have looked, as well as acted, the part that we were playing — a few things from Peter's flat and we were off… sandwiches, a flask of tea, tired, but happy, we made our last removal trip down to Somerset.

On arrival in Somerset, the back of the van would not open, fortunately… I say this, because by asking our neighbours in the garden flat if they knew how to open it… which they did… they also very kindly helped us unload the van *upstairs*, which was no mean feat. Like most people moving, you wonder what you are going to do with everything, and how many years it will take to get yourself straight; deciding it was all too much for one *long* day, we put a mattress down on the floor and slept… and slept… and slept.

The following day we awoke in our *new home*.

When you go along with life's plan for you, everything goes well, and so it did with the furniture and curtains; everything fitted into place perfectly. Everything was just the correct size, tables went into corners, there were picture hooks where we wanted our pictures to hang and the only thing we did not have, were curtains to fit the fifteen foot windows and side windows in the lounge — we made these at a later date.

Ansford Inn was situated within half a mile of Castle Cary, by the main road. Its courtyard backed onto playing fields with only one small house standing in the corner of the courtyard and behind this, there was a large piece of waste land. The house beyond this belonged to Jim and Pauline Allen; over the main road, lived the owners of the Inn in their own large house and garden.

The Inn had been turned into five large flats. The three downstairs flats were occupied by a young couple, a Mrs Marjorie Scutt, who lived on her own, since her husband died and who had the flat immediately below us and a further couple with a grown up son. There was one empty flat adjoining us, but for now, nothing registered in our minds except getting the flat habitable. Meanwhile, though Mrs Hiscock and Susan were extremely welcoming, we found it was like 'pioneering' with the local residents.

While we had been visitors, we presented no threat to them, but now we had taken up residence in Ansford, which is a different community to Castle Cary, we did present a threat… who are these people from London? People who came from there were found to be unfriendly and haughty and tried to boss them about. As for being healers — what are healers? even then, healing was not known in Somerset, except to a minority. One morning, I invited a neighbour to have coffee with me; her reply was, "You will have to wait until I ask you," and this typifies how things were. In most small country villages and towns, there is an enormous amount of interbreeding, and from this, several large families stick out in the community and are respected. Like any other interbreeding of humans or animals, it quite often has an adverse effect, so although understanding the whole situation, it did not make it any easier for us at the time.

On finalising our commitments in London, we now settled down to a new lifestyle. With the money that had been given to me, we realised we could live for a while, without getting too concerned. We needed a rest after all the working and planning that had had to take priority to a holiday.

"Peter, let's take a fortnight away, somewhere," I said, "We need some sea air."

"Where can we go?" Peter said, adding "I am certain we should try to save the money we have and not have a holiday."

"We need the break together," I replied, "And money is meant to be spent, providing it is spent wisely; we do need time to rest, and talk… to sort out our next step."

At last, Peter agreed and we took off to Cornwall. We found a hotel in Polzeath and we were spoilt for a whole fortnight. I suppose one could say it was our honeymoon for in spirit we were already married… by a priest… not yet. We spoke of getting married in a church, or Registry office for the families sakes, and because of our work at that time, it was demanded of us — not so these days. Joan and Peter had already applied for a divorce, on the grounds of incompatibility. Bert was not being very co-operative with me in this matter and so to avoid any unpleasantness for anyone, I said that we should wait for two years and then I could automatically get a divorce. In my eyes, Peter and I had promised, and made our vows to each other a long time ago, so we could both wait and then set the seal for *mortal reasons* only, after two years had elapsed.

I was wearing the engagement ring that Peter had bought Irene, his first wife; it was beautiful and a privilege to wear.

"Could I have a wedding ring?" I asked.

"When we are married." He replied.

"But we are, aren't we?" I asked in dismay.

"Of course." said Peter and a very old ring with much history to it was found not long after.

I could not walk very well, now. The past weeks had taken their toll; after only a few steps I would have to sit, my whole body was aching and sleep was difficult. We spent our time talking, reading and playing cards (which my brothers had taught me). The sea air felt good on our faces and short outings, combined with healing, slowly built me up again. Soon, we were on our way home.

24

Time for a Cure

ON our return, my health started to deteriorate again. I knew Peter's mother felt my time of passing was near. I wondered why this was happening now. Before I had left London, the Doctor had told me on my last visit for a check–up and x–ray that I had diverticulitis. "You can't die from it," he said, "But watch your diet, you will just have to live with it." Now, with this, my back, neck, an arm that now would not move and a feeling within me that felt like a 'dropped womb', what use was I... only a burden.

Shortly after our arrival back, sitting in our lounge one day while Peter was out, I heard a voice say, "Rena" — I looked up and saw an empty space; once more a voice said, "Rena," and though seeing no one, I remembered my experience with TB[13] and said quietly, "What do you want?"

"It is time for you to be made whole," this voice said.

Feeling this would be a major miracle and pretty well impossible, I said, "Who are you?"

"Never mind who I am, just listen. Tell Peter he must give you a healing tonight; let me speak through you and guide him through what he has to do — you will not be able to get up for three days after this operation."

"What operation?" I asked, getting concerned.

"Your womb is not in its right place and your colon has pockets in it."

"Is this to take place all at once?" I asked.

"Yes, it is time, but you must do everything I ask you to."

I then asked him again, who he was, for I knew it was a man's voice.

"You are persistent, but quite right to be," he said "I am Chin Sen Lu and I am here to help you get better, you have a lot of work to do yet."

"Why can't Peter do it himself?" I asked.

"It is something beyond his ability at present." he said.

I finally stopped asking questions when I had been told it was meant for me to suffer all these things, there was a purpose that I would be shown later. But now, the time of suffering was over and it was time for the body to be made ready for further work of a spiritual nature.

Not really believing all this and yet hoping I was not dreaming, or even making it up, I told Peter of the conversation with the person called Chin Sen Lu; he believed it straight away and what took place that evening was very strange to me. All I remember is being woken up with a voice saying, "It is finished." I could not get up and I felt as though I had come out of an anaesthetic — very drowsy.

Peter carried me to bed and I had my first good night's sleep for a long time. On waking, I knew exactly what had to be done, as though my information had been received in my sleep state.

"Please put my feet higher than my head." I said, "I must have only liquids, nothing else for three days and no movement must be made with the lower part of me." I continued.

Peter had already made up a special bed for me in the lounge so we could be together during the daytime; he also, without knowing it, put my bed facing East. When my body came out of its anaesthetic state, it went through all the normal steps of recovery, which are not pleasant. This, I know, was a further learning and development for me; also, my body was extremely tired and could not take a sudden change to a perfect state — it had to be gradual. Whenever I went to do anything I should not do, Chin Sen Lu was there; it was like having a permanent consultant and surgeon at my bedside at all times. Some of our conversations were quite humorous,

"I need to go to the toilet." I said to Peter.

"No, you do not." said Chin Sen Lu — no I didn't.

"Ask Peter to bring the bedpan." said Chin Sen Lu.

"I don't need it." I said — oh, yes I did!

At the end of the three days and nights, I was allowed up for ten minutes, then the next day twenty minutes and so each day I felt, and became stronger. I kept the knowledge of the operation to myself, but I knew my first experience of true spiritual healing had taken place and the Soul that came to help, I know to be a true friend who, like a friend, would often talk to me to lighten the passing days.

There is no divide between the planes, only that which we make ourselves.

Master Meditation
and
Master Life

25

The Start of a Centre

"RENA, where are you?" called Peter. "I am in the kitchen." I said as I walked out of the door into the round landing. "Where are you?" said Peter again.

"Looking for you." I said, going through a further door.

"Please will you stand still!" said Peter, who had gone through a third door and not found me. Now, this happened often and became an amusing game to play, if I wanted to tease him.

"I have heard the flat next door is for let;" he told me, "It's only a few pounds extra, shall we take it and start our healing there?"

"Wonderful." I replied.

The flat next to ours consisted of one large room and an extra large long room, plus a kitchen and bathroom. The rent was low because it needed a great deal of work done on it, the flat had been empty for some time and all the rooms needed decorating. We had a partition made and put up, in the smaller room, thereby giving us two cubicles to do our healings in. The large room was made into a waiting room which was also used for our meditation and prayer times. The colours used for each of these rooms chose themselves; each time we went to buy a particular colour… it would get changed, in our minds, to another colour we would never have thought of choosing. Work on the second flat was finished in a few weeks.

Then, there were the visiting cards to think about; to begin with, we used our own names on pale blue cards, we also advertised in the shop windows that were used for that purpose. The money we now had was not sufficient to take advertising space in the local papers, so we mentioned it in town to shopkeepers and acquaintances.

The money had almost run out; we decided that one of us should build up the healing side, while the other one should get a job. Peter said he felt he should get the job and I take the healing until we were busy enough for him to join me. There was a notice in the local paper advertising a baker's round in Castle Cary — Peter went for an interview and got the job; he was to be up at five o'clock and not return until his round was finished.

Only people who have had any connection with bakers rounds, can know just how many prices of cakes, bread and pies there are to remember, plus all the different types, as well. We had a rehearsal that night — I asked Peter the price of each cake and bread and he told me; he learnt the prices quickly, but was I glad it was not me!

He would go down the road each day imitating Charlie Chaplin's walk, to make me laugh.

He would bring home lovely fresh cakes and bread — sometimes he would be back very late, but he always put down his basket and picked up a tea towel to give me a hand. His tales of biting dogs, work–worn women, friendly farmers and runaway horses that he enticed with biscuits, would fill a book on their own. Meanwhile, as the customers got to know Peter, he would tell them he was a healer and this helped to dispel an enormous amount of ignorance about healing, and patients started coming to us with their problems.

The healing built up slowly, but surely, and I loved every minute of it. We were earning enough money now to pay our way.

When healing in London at S.A.G.B., no charge was made to patients for the healings, there was a donation plate. Peter also never charged when he used to give healings at home, but patients never seemed to appreciate this, at least, only a few did, the rest would arrive late, or not at all, or they would cancel saying they had a hair appointment half an hour before they were due to come.

For this reason, we decided to make a charge for our *time* only, on a sliding scale basis, which has worked very well, ever since and brings self–respect and appreciation with it. Many times we would visit and heal for no payment whatsoever and quite often we received butter, vegetables or home made cakes as payment… which was wonderful, but we had to have some money to enable us to live… to enable us to heal.

You
are
God

26

Spiritual Unfoldments

*T*HERE are many lovely walks around Ansford where one can go and not meet anyone; my walks would take me there whenever I had time to spare. As a child, we had holidays on farms and our first house was in the country, so at heart I have always been a 'country girl'. Growing up afterwards in towns, for a great part of my life, it was sad to discover how many flowers, trees and shrubs there were whose names I could not remember.

It was not long after starting on these walks that I would get strange feelings to look at certain places, and on doing so, would discover a beautiful plant, unusual butterfly, or an unusually coloured stone. I did not think too hard about these feelings, until one day my hand felt as though it was being held. I moved my fingers, but still felt something there. Having a very vivid imagination, yet at the same time being a 'very down to earth person', my first reaction was, "Don't be silly", my second, "To find out about the feeling". I heard an unheard, "chuckle".

"Don't worry, I'm Rydal and I thought this was the best way of making myself known."

"Why are you here?" I ventured to ask.

"I have been asked to bring back your memory of the countryside, to show you certain spiritual rules and ways in life that you were aware of in your past life."

Now, I had heard of reincarnation, but was not sure I believed in it; he heard my mind's thoughts and replied. "It is not for me to tell you about these things, only to guide you in this next step."

"I only want you if you are of God." I said.

Chuckling once more, he said, "I am of God." And so a friendship was formed that lasted over a year.

I knew so little of the different planes of life, energy and incarnation, that there were many things to learn about. Rydal was a good tutor; he showed me the difference in the grasses, he taught me how one could converse with animals — "But I know this," I said, "I remember doing this before... somewhere."

"Yes, I am only here for recall purposes." Rydal replied, "Now let me show you how to see through buildings."

I laughed, "That is impossible." I said.

"Nothing is impossible, there is no such word, only does it seem so in the minds of people." Rydal, after saying these words, showed and brought back this memory to me.

"Why do I need to know this? I am not the sort of person to want to look through buildings." I was determined there must be a good reason for doing this, otherwise it did not interest me at all. Saying this to Rydal, he asked me to accept these happenings, unconditionally, for I was a person who would only learn by practical experience, not by being told, and in the future, very soon, everything would be revealed to me.

He reminded me about Aranti, saying she had brought back my life, with her, in ancient Greece, the temple and the initiations I had experienced, bringing back my ability to read dreams and see the future — when to use it and how to be master of it. "Yes," I replied, "But I have not used it since."

"No," Rydal said, "It is not time, let us enjoy our walks; listen to me, all will be shown to you, in due course; beware of telling this to anyone, but Peter."

These tutorial walks continued, and I now looked forward to them, eagerly awaiting my next insight into matters at present unknown to me.

One day, Rydal did not make himself known and I was very sad. I had a feeling to go over to the field next to the footpath, so I went, climbing over a stile into a further field — I saw a lovely horse and spoke to it, as taught me, and the piebald horse came trotting over to me; we conversed silently until it was time for me to go. It had been a lovely day, but where was Rydal? The following day, on my walk, Rydal did make himself known.

"Did you enjoy yourself yesterday?" he asked.

"It was an unusual day." I replied, and told him all about the horse and my conversing with it; of course he already knew of these happenings but did not say so as such — "so you find what I say is true?"

"Yes," I replied, "but did you arrange it?"

"Yes, I did," he said, "Also, not to be with you."

"Why did you do that?" I asked.

"You must not expect these things to happen, or look forward to them, please accept them as normal, to happen when they need to." He went on to say, "I want you to see that this approach to life is how people used to be; most people have lost this art in exchange for more mortal pursuits, and though it will come back quickly in time, to people, I want you to know that it can be done *now*. Live in the moment of time, accept these happenings as normal, but be in charge of them at all times."

I wanted to ask many more questions, but I knew that it was not the time for any more.

As our Centre grew, with patients, so my training continued, with pleasant surprises coming, I believe, as a treat. I tried not to take Rydal or my learning for granted, to accept them as normal, so when one day, on our walk Rydal informed me his work with me was finished, I took this with the knowledge that he would always be there if I really needed him… as normal.

Many wonderful days had been mine, with untold treasures being recaptured, many happenings and talks of the future, with Rydal, that in the following chapters, will unfold and tell themself.

The Centre was very busy now; I had also taken in a girl named Jane, who needed a home — she had many problems of which one was overeating. I loved her very much and wanted her to become part of our family, but it was not to be; the turmoil within her was too much for us to handle and it became very disruptive… whatever we tried to do. We had to be firm… to be kind and she went back to live with her Uncle. As this episode finished, another began.

*All our problems are good
for us
There are no bad ones*

27

Another Breast

ONE morning, on opening the post, I found a letter addressed to myself, from the Wincanton Hospital, suggesting an appointment time for me. This was very unusual as I had not seen a Doctor, or been to a hospital for some time now; my interest took me to the appointment.

The receptionist was very surprised at my ignorance of why I was there. Showing her the letter, she seemed even more concerned and asked me to wait while she went in search of the Doctor. Soon, I was ushered into a small room where the Doctor — I assumed he was a Doctor, asked me to take a seat apologising for the lack of information in the letter that was sent to me. He then proceeded to ask me if I would like a transplant for my second breast.

I was taken aback… for a long time ago, Chin Sen Lu had told me there would be a possibility of a new breast; not knowing what he meant and not having time to think about it, the conversation had erased itself from my thoughts… now, this is what he meant! I allowed an examination to follow, wondering if this was something I should consider for Peter's sake. No problem here Mrs Denton, the Doctor was saying, there is sufficient tissue here to make a good job of it. He went on to explain that a cut would be made and a silicon bag of gel would be inserted under the skin and the skin then placed over the top; a nipple could be added if I wished.

The whole idea of what he was explaining to me horrified me, but I thanked him for his thoughts and left rather rapidly, feeling only partly what it must be like to be a *guinea pig*.

Arriving home, I told Peter of my visit to the hospital and asked him what he thought of me having this operation — would he like me to? Peter did not think very long, as some people might do, but said, "No, definitely not… I love you as you are and for what you are; ring the hospital and say no to them". I was very relieved to hear his answer, but I knew I had to ask him.

Soon after this, the new silicon prosthesis came into being and this, I believe, helped a great deal of women come to terms with the loss of a breast or breasts.

This is a vast subject and each must act according to their beliefs. Our belief is that implants are not natural, so therefore there is always a risk.

It is our choice to take that risk or not.

28

Natural Happenings

*T*HERE were times, during these difficult years, when in great need, Ji Jesus would cradle my head on his lap and speak to me lovingly, of the trials in life. Of his crucifix time, not on the cross of wood, but the cross of people not listening… the misunderstanding and hate that people had borne him as he went about his life's work. He told me that my work to come would mean enduring, in the same way, with few people understanding, so my strength of faith must be great.

These times when he spoke were very beautiful; I know he has appeared to many people when they have needed consoling, and why not, bearing in mind the different facets of ourselves and the 'Spirit's' ability to travel.

My mother would tell me of a friend in South Africa that she had visited in her 'wakeful' state — she spoke of different species of flowers, the steps leading down to a pond and what the friend was doing at that time, all this being confirmed in writing by the person themself.

One time, after one of my spiritual operations, during my recuperation when I was in pain and feeling very tired, I fell into a wakeful state whereby I was taken down to the Ganges by someone, who helped me bathe then wrapped my body round and round with a cloth that made me feel like a 'mummy', then my body was lain in a hammock to rest. When I fully returned to consciousness, my bodily pain had disappeared completely.

There is a purpose behind all seeing, whether one is dreaming, or in the mid–between stage of sleep and awake, called the Wakeful state — in all these different stages, we can make progress.

I have seen my mother, my dog Captain that passed, my unborn son. I have flown over buildings knowingly controlling the flight; I have travelled at night and known of my travels on awakening. A Pixie has spoken to me and I have visited cathedrals and wars, yet that is just the tip of the many spiritual levels, or mansions, that there are, and also of our abilities.

This is no made–up story; many experiences like this have been felt by many people, for a long time. We need to know… have more knowledge about our deeper *SELVES*. Know that *these* are *normal happenings not abnormal* and that we need not be afraid of them. We must ask and use prayers as our advancement, then whatever follows will come naturally, but if we push to gain entry to such happenings, *then* and only *then* should we fear.

My time has not yet come to divulge more, working on the principle that those who know will understand and those who do not, will either decide, or perhaps take time to *think*. What happens in our lives is given to prepare and strengthen us for our next step and in my case it was to teach me — so I could teach others… from experience… not purely from hearsay.

The Pixie that came to speak to me has an unusual story to it and taught me a lesson in belief. Hearing of Pixies, Fairies and Gnomes that lived in gardens and woodland areas, was one thing… but to believe it… was another. The desire to believe in these 'little folk' was within me… the belief… was not.

One of my chief delights, in times of stress, was to picture myself as a large bird, flying and perching on the top of the largest tree we had in our garden and then look and listen to the sounds of life around me. One day I was sitting in the garden, deep in contemplation, when a small voice said, "What a funny person you are, wanting to fly to the tops of trees".

I realised a Pixie was talking to me and asked, "Do you live in trees and flowers?"

"Among the trees." He replied.

"Do you play?" I ventured to ask.

"Sometimes, with the Elves, though usually I work creating vibrations of strength for the various trees around."

I *had* to ask him. "Do you wear a red hat?"

He laughed, "Why should I? No, I don't, only a leaf sometimes on my head!" Then he started to sing in rhyme fashion; I heard Peter calling me from the house and as he did so, the Pixie left and now knowing, beyond all doubt, that Pixies exist, I returned to the house.

Past is experience
Future is only ideas
The Now is for living

29

Peter ~ Home

WE were busy now with so many new patients that I could not cope on my own any longer. I had tried to carry on myself, as it was a difficult time for Peter to leave the Bakery, but my instinct told me it was them or me; we had also heard that Peter's Uncle in Exmouth had passed. We had been visiting him every week up to then — he was a dear cantankerous old man, whom I loved and respected; his hair and nails would be my weekly job and he loved to 'pull my leg', on all matters, when he could. Uncle Harry would mention our name to people in Exmouth and we ended up seeing patients there on our day out. We eventually started a one day clinic in Exmouth, which lasted several months.

"Peter, please will you give in your notice?" I asked him, "Not only do I feel ill with the workload, but you have to see to your Uncle's estate and we have also to put the vegetable garden into production."

Peter gave up his baker's round.

The vegetable garden came to us by asking Mrs Hiscock if we could rent her waste ground; it was easily sixty feet by forty feet or more, and we wanted to produce our own fresh organic vegetables. "Yes," she said, "But it will need some digging." It did.

We took a small portion of it to make a patio and flower garden, the rest we sowed with all different types of vegetables and herbs, with a small partition between the patio and vegetable patch.

Things were happening quickly now.

The lower garden flat below our healing room became vacant — we took it. This flat had one bedroom, large lounge, kitchen, bathroom and toilet. It was a light and airy flat, once more let to us at a very reasonable rent. Now we could have patients to stay with us, to recuperate, or just for a rest. The lounge had a lovely old fireplace where logs were burnt and problems forgotten.

We then decided after much talking and giving the subject a great deal of thought, that we should call the Centre "The Denton Healing Centre", and we would have a sign erected by the entrance into the courtyard, facing on to the road. This was a good idea, except when local school children were in high spirits, they would raise the sign from the ground, leaving it in evidence for us to put in again.

I knew this Centre was to be Peter's, for now, as I had already had my own Clinic. I was to be a backup, as well as a partner, but not take the lead. This seemed right and just to me; I accepted the position willingly.

We had a problem arise from erecting the sign — the postman happened to be on the Parish Council and rang the Town Planning Department asking whether we had planning permission for healing to be carried out on the premises. A representative from the Department called on us to discuss the matter; he told us that we had to fill in an application for permission to be given to use the flat for healing. This took us by surprise as we did not have to do this in London — apparently certain counties did differ from each other at that time.

After a lot of 'red tape' and weeks after our application, permission was granted.

Now, we were not only healing each day, but also having people to stay, full board, as well as three flats and garden maintenance to see to. One person who came to stay, while her mother had a holiday, was suffering from an inhibiting physical disease. Her mother, when booking her in advance, said she could walk; it turned out that she needed someone with her most of the twenty–four hours and could hardly move. We had to stoke the fire during the night and be there for her — we had no bells in those days linking the flats together, so she could not ring for us, and that fortnight was the longest one I had ever known.

I asked her if I might try her wheelchair, and stayed in it for a while, to experience what it must be like to be bound to one. The girl (whose name I will not mention), liked being looked after and gave no sign of wanting to recover. This was a good lesson for me, for the future and taught me to ask a lot more questions before people came to stay with us.

Now that the sign was up I said, "Let's send out invitations to professional people, to come and have a discussion with us."

Peter said, "What a good idea" and we sent out fifty invitations. We invited them to come and debate with us about each other so that we could learn from each other and we could tell them what we believed in. On the day in question, only twelve turned up and only twenty acknowledged our invitations. We had three clergymen, a Matron, a Doctor, Pauline Allen, who was Deputy Headmistress of the Primary School, a Headmistress from a nearby large Private School — Mrs Churchouse, a Farmer and David from Castle Cary Bakeries along with several other interested parties including Reverend Casley from the local Methodist Church.

We held the discussion downstairs, with comfortable chairs set out, a large table with sandwiches and cakes and a choice of liquid intake, ready prepared — It was a success, with all agreeing that healing was needed, but begging to differ when and why it should be given. The Doctor present, wished to come again and learn more… as time only permitted touching the perimeter of healing matters. The Reverend Casley was very forthcoming and added a great deal to the afternoon. There were many good 'comebacks' from this discussion.

I only write this to show how important these meetings are — time consuming to prepare, but invaluable for the future.

Mine Eye
is
my delight

30

Gall–Stone Time

"PETER, I'm sorry, I must go to bed straight away." I had been suffering pain on and off for a few weeks now, and it seemed as though it was all coming to a head. It was, fortunately for us, a free day, so no one would be let down by my taking time off. I had a gallstone… this I knew, I also knew that it would be passed in due course without any medical treatment, except healings.

I also knew there were healings to be given the following day and we were both fully booked. Musing this over, while making my way to bed, I could not help but smile — even with the pain — and wonder how the powers were going to sort this out. My struggling with the coming and going of the intense pain was only made bearable by the fact of knowing it had to happen this way and that I would be *healing again tomorrow;* I had been told this by Chin Sen Lu and such was my faith, I knew it was so. After seventeen hours or more, using my breathing techniques to get me through, I suddenly felt very exhausted; if I could only sleep, or enter into the samadhi state… but there was no energy for these things.

I felt a need to call the Doctor for something to make me sleep. "Tell him, I am fine, it's only a gallstone and will pass soon, but I need my energies for tomorrow's work." I said to Peter. He rang him and within half an hour, he was with me giving me an injection, like it or not, in my *derrière;* I remember no more except saying, "Please do not bother to come back tomorrow."

When he did turn up the following morning, early, we both got a surprise, me to see him and he to see I was as 'good as new' and ready for the day. We have had a mutual respect for each other ever since.

So, that's how the powers wanted it!

Love
is
The One

31

Preparation for a Guru

IN the evenings, at home, we would listen to music, read, write or plan for the next day; in fine weather, we would be in the garden. Having no television seemed strange to our new friends, but was a sheer delight to us; we never missed it at all. I found I was writing poems, songs and recording music, to the best of my limitations — all to be used in the future. My body was strong enough now, to do any work that was demanded of me.

In the evenings, by the fire, we would sit quietly, closing our eyes and listening to light orchestral music. I would find, some evenings, that a soul… my mother… my father or little John would make themselves felt and known to me. After prayer time in the evenings, I would be aware of 'lost souls' needing help and would find ways of helping them, by showing them 'how to find the light' — all natural to me and only later on in my life did I realise… it was called… *rescue work* and also, *specialised work.*

We had a lovely male ghost in Ansford Inn, he smoked a pipe in the rooms where we sat at night, until I informed him that his pipe was not good for our health; he would then only smoke in the toilet. He would come for car rides with us and did not seem in a hurry to leave us, so we accepted him, asking him not to make himself known to others that came and not to smoke at those times — he agreed and we all lived happily together. Not all souls want to leave this earth plane straight away, but in due course, they do… as our friend did.

Peter wondered if we could ask for a group of Soul Brothers to give us advice; I agreed to ask, and was told this would be done, if we needed it, and that we must try to sit at a given time and on a set day. We held these meetings each week — there were six of us including ourselves and we gained a great deal of information on the running of the Centre from these meetings. I knew their names and forms and many a humorous time was spent with them, when more important matters were finalised; I only wish Peter could have seen them as I did.

Peter's strength lies in his utter faith. He does not see, hear or feel when he is healing, but he is still a powerful healer and does not doubt the power within, which to my mind is a wonderful gift in itself. He had grown up in a healing atmosphere and he was, rightly, called Peter *THE ROCK*.

After a few months, I said to Peter that I felt our Brothers group was no longer called for. We now had to commune more with our higher selves as this was what was wanted of us. We all disbanded, knowing and realising the power of our own minds and selves.

I now found I had no problem with adjusting to the different levels in life — my spiritual healing became yet another part of my life.

My food intake was small, my prayer and silent times became longer; I knew now, what I had wanted and always, unknowingly, wanted:

A GURU TO ENLIGHTEN ME AND
BRING ME TO FRUITION ~
but would I find ONE?

32

My Guru

*T*HE library in Castle Cary, is small, but adequate for the town's needs, and my love of reading books often took me there, where I would feast my eyes on many books, taking only one or two away with me, as it took me several weeks to read them, owing to our busy schedule.

On one particular day, Peter was going in to get a book and although I went along with him, I was not particularly interested as I still had a book at home to finish and was not in the mood for browsing.

"There's a book there you might like to read." Peter said, looking in the direction of the autobiographies. I did not want to be bothered, but went over to the section out of politeness, to have a look. Looking at several, one book that was almost falling out over the bookcase, caught my eye. I pushed it back alongside the others, feeling little energy within to make me pursue it further... and yet... I could not move away — or out of the library, something was holding me there. Absent–mindedly, my feet returned me to the book shelf; putting my hand out, I took a book out — the very one I had pushed back. The photograph held me and I turned to Peter to show it to him, "That's the book I thought you might like", he said.

Somehow... by now, I could feel an excitement growing within me, a surging of desire, of an unknown nature. This is silly... what is happening to me... this feeling must be curbed; doing just this, I duly took the book out and put it in my shopping bag and thought no more about it until later that evening, when the opportunity to retire early came, and we took it.

I picked up the book *Autobiography of a Yogi* and looking once more at the picture, felt the same surge of excitement as before… I started to read. As I read and turned each page, my feelings of knowing this Yogi and others became very strong; what was written about, seemed natural. Peter spoke to me several times and although I was aware of sounds, my eyes and mind were captured by the writings.

My thoughts were on how fortunate Yogananda was to have found his Guru; I had yearned for a 'dispeller of darkness', a 'Guru' for so long now… I had even thought of travelling to India, or abroad somewhere to find one, believing that they must live there, as I had not heard of one here. How could I find one? — was I ready, or even worthy of one? With all these restless questions unanswered, I closed the book and as I turned my head away from Peter towards the wall, still awake, I saw a boy with golden hair and a most beautiful face, smiling at me; then I noticed an upright, Eastern faced man with a beard; his eyes held a steady, firm gaze as he looked towards me and then I saw the face of Yogananda, the man on the cover of the book I was reading.

I shook my head and blinked my eyes — they were there for a fraction longer, then floated away, disintegrating into light and then into nothingness and it seemed that the wall had swallowed them up. I did not believe what I had seen, yet I was not asleep. I decided sleep would be the best thing to rectify my 'hallucinations'.

"Time to get up," a clear voice said. Being three quarters still asleep, and believing it to be Peter that spoke, I turned, looked at the clock which said 3am and replied, "Not yet, it's not morning", and promptly turned on my side to continue my sleep.

"It's time to get up, come into the Meditation room." This time I woke up; Peter was asleep, snoring soundly. Wondering, and curious as to what was going on, I made my way, in darkness, to the room and turning on the light, looked around — no one there I thought to myself, although it would be pleasant to meditate now for a little while, so turning the light off, with a candle lit, I sat on a chair and with closed eyes was just about to say a prayer, when this voice came again.

"So you are here" — just a voice.

"Well, yes." I said, feeling somewhat a fool.

"I have had to wait a long time for you to be ready in your development — you had to have many experiences given to you and more earthly remembrances before I could come to you," this voice continued.

"What for?" I asked him.

"For you to go through the fire of life before I could come to you." His voice was gentle, but firm as he spoke, "You wanted a Guru, I am here."

"But, I can't see You."

"You did see me a little while ago."

"Then, why can't I see you now?" I asked.

"Sometimes it is best to communicate with you like this because if you came into a room and found someone sitting there at this time, would it not scare you?" He was telling me rather than asking me. Yes, there was truth in what he said.

"Are you truly my Guru?"

"Yes, I am and we have much to do; each morning I will wake you up at the same time, or earlier sometimes and I want you to come and sit here with me. Soon, I will show myself, but till then I want you to know I am your Guru Yogananda and I have been delegated the wondrous task of opening your lotus petals, until you are in full bloom. I will teach you that which you need to know — bless you my child — go now."

On hearing *HIM* say this, I could not reply — it felt like a dream. Yes, I was used to spirit souls contacting me, but this was either a hoax or the real thing — may I be forgiven now for ever doubting.

Each morning I was awoken as told and each morning I responded by putting a gown over night attire and joining the person in the Meditation room. It took some time before I was convinced of the presence and truth of a Guru.

I had finished the book by now and many questions came hurriedly out of my mouth; he gave me proof of his existence, knowing that I needed it and sometimes I would see his face, but as our meetings continued and my love and devotion for him with it, nothing else mattered except that he was feeding me knowledge of a kind that I had yearned for... for a long time.

He spoke to me about the deeper spiritual knowledge and of meditation. He sat with me in half lotus position while knowing that my legs would have to get used to the full lotus position. He showed me exercises to keep me supple, while teaching me the ancient breathing that he wished me to have knowledge of. Most of the things he was teaching me I felt that I had done before somewhere and I asked him if this was true; he said, "I am awakening the memories within you," and he seemed to read my thoughts and continued saying, "You have known ascetic life before, as a landowner".

"As a man or a woman?" I asked.

"A man, who spent his life serving God."

"Was he English?"

"No, no, and no more questions now — let us talk about the scriptures," and he continued expanding on all the subjects I had ever wondered about.

One morning I asked him if the S.R.F.[14] in America would believe these happenings and could I tell them? His answer was no, they would say it was dreamt or made up and that I must not tell anyone — yet — except Peter. "But, why me?" I asked, "Surely there must be others who would have complete faith straight away and would not a man be better for the task you have in mind for me?"

Now, Yoganandaji[15], as I now called him, had told me that my path would be difficult, with many responsibilities; people would disbelieve and turn away from the love and the light and that everything I had been through was for the benefit of souls who would come my way in the future. This is why I asked this question. His answer to my questions were that "a woman who would not hurt a fly and with an abundance of love, was needed and that strong faith came from testing it... not from blind faith." As I was thinking — H'mm, I wish I had more beauty of face to attract more souls. He chuckled adding, "You have everything you need, if you had more, people would come to look at you and not listen to you; you are hidden, for those to find you who are ready within for further progress, and need you". On hearing these words, I felt very humble and asked his forgiveness for doubting his judgement.

I had never forgotten reading in his book, that Guruji had worn a bangle that had been given to him, a very spiritual one. I had nothing like this from my Guru and one day I asked him if I could have a bangle to wear... always... to remind me of him. "Soon," was his reply, "But not yet, there is still more work to be done."

Our meetings had taken place regularly, for nearly a year now. Each morning at three a.m till six or seven a.m. I would sit and listen, spellbound, asking questions, though not as many as I used to. Sometimes, if I had done well, the Master's voice would become extra loving and now the bond between us was as it should be between Disciple and Guru — my humbly loving him with deep respect, yet feeling he loved me as well.

I had to go to London for several days, on business; would it be all right to miss my instruction? I asked Guruji. "You may, but hurry back – you will enjoy yourself." What did he know that I did not?...

It was pouring with rain in London on the afternoon I had arranged to meet Trudy, for my daughter and I to have a few hours together. Knowing Trudy well enough to know she did not like the rain, I suggested we could go home to her house and talk over a 'cuppa', but no... she had other plans.

"We are going to Covent Garden." She said.

"Why?" I asked.

"I don't really know," was her reply, her attitude was one I recognised well as that of a person doing something of a spiritual nature, without being totally aware of it. Seeing this, we took our seats, though wet through, on a bus heading for Covent Garden. Alighting there, we made our way to the market. Once there I felt compelled to go to a particular stall... and there I found a bracelet that was for me — it was made of copper, brass and had a gold thread finish. "That's for you." I heard Guruji say. I tried it on, it fitted perfectly and although there were others there, this was the only one that 'called' to me. Then Trudy said an unusual thing, "I can't buy this bracelet for you, you must get it for yourself". I wonder to this day if she ever found out the true significance to that whole journey.

On my return home I could hardly wait till three o'clock the following morning. When it came time for my meeting with Guruji, I was in there extra early to tell him all about my journey and show him the bracelet; of course he had already seen it a long time before I did. The money for it came in an unusual way — a present from an unknown source. Well, I was happy now and so was Guruji with one less 'gentle demand' from his devotee.

I found out that very few people called my Guru, Paramahansaji[16] which is a name that he liked, so in trying to show my great respect for him, I started to call him by this name.

"And I shall give you the names 'Mata Yogananda'," he said, "Mata — Mother, as you are the spiritual mother of the Centre and the Centres you will have, and 'Yogananda', because of your bliss and oneness with God." My joy knew no bounds on hearing him give me these names, for they are not given lightly.

I fell to my knees, and asked that I may always be worthy of them.

One day I asked him if it was necessary for people to seek their Gurus in Eastern countries. His face and voice took on a sad expression as he told me of the 'heartache' that there would be in these countries, the uprisings that would have to happen before they could ever claim spiritual sovereignty again. He went on to say that there is no need for people to search outside their own country, or maybe even their 'hometown'. When the correct time in their evolutionary stage of life had been reached, and with their desire aflame within themselves to go forward, then they would meet a teacher, or if more advanced still, a Guru.

"If it is a Guru," he went on to say, "He will recognise the one sent to him, but not necessarily will the disciple recognise his Guru, for each disciple has a preconceived idea of what they would like, starting with the outward looks, but this, in reality, never works out well, and sometimes a devotee will dismiss even the thought of their teacher, or Guru, because they have not got the gender, or looks they feel they should have." " Do remember," he continued, "There are many teachers that can teach us many things, but Gurus are more specialised in their field and are Self–Realized beings, who only come for a very special *task* to be done." I thanked him for this explanation and we then sat in meditation together before he departed.

My life now, was one of complete bliss and peace, with my healing work in the daytime, my long meditations and then my meetings with my Guru. These times satisfied all my mortal and spiritual hungers and my feeling of being at one with all of life – such unconditional love for all of God's creatures, made me want to help others, so much, but there were a few more steps to take yet before I was ready for this to happen.

Guruji had a special poem he loved called *The Hound of Heaven;* I wanted to speak this on to a tape, so that I could play it sometimes before we met in the morning. While making this very inadequate recording, Guruji wafted the most beautiful perfume into the room, Peter and myself could smell this sweet perfume, but an Uncle of ours who was in the room with us, could not sense the smell at all. Such are the wonders in life.

My lack of any desire for material wants and my eating of much less food became apparent to our friends. Seeing my peace and happiness being so complete, they would sometimes try to question me on the cause of this change. Not being allowed to tell them, I would try to change the subject; more often than not, I would read their minds before they asked me and so the issue was bypassed.

The meditative state that I now found myself to be in at all times, gave a clarity of thought and action that made my work and play extra beautiful, at the same time as my perceptions of everything and everyone around me grew out of all proportion. This responsibility of seeing and knowing can hurt us, unless one is trained and without ego, then you know the truth of what people are thinking and doing and there is no hurt, just acknowledgement of them... as they are.

"Let thine eye be single, lest it be plucked from thee, for it shall perceive and know, for our mortal eyes can deceive us as well as our ears". Our having a third eye, a reflection of the pituitary gland which is in the middle of the brow, is no fairy story — it exists to be used and the knowledge of these and many more important things were now being shown and taught to me. The imagination is the beginning of manifestation and can become reality. Full ability to concentrate on *anything* that we need to, at any given time, is a much needed accomplishment; we had it as a child, losing it as we grew into adulthood.

To know that *we are all sons and daughters of the UNIVERSAL power* and not one of us is loved *more* or *less* than the other. As I listened and absorbed, the words spoken to me sounded so logical, down to earth... and *TRUE.*

Paramahansaji was talking to me one morning, telling me that one day I, too, would become a Guru and that when that day came, I must accept the mantle. He also told me I would visit America one day soon — this prompted a flood of questions from me, but he would not be drawn to answer any of them and continued, saying that he would eventually like me to call the Centre the Self-Realization Healing Centre, but that the change must come about slowly. I said I had started calling the Centre the Denton Healing Centre as I felt it should be, this he was pleased with, leaving it to us to make the full name change when the right time had come to do so.

"Soon, you will not be needing me," he added, "Then you must practise all you have been taught, remembering that you are meant to work with pure love and wisdom at all times; keep your intuitiveness high within, for that is the guiding light — if you try to conform to the standards of a more mortal nature, you will find that you will not be happy."

His words saddened me, to think that soon our meetings would cease and I asked him if he would be there if I ever needed him.

"Yes, my child, but only if you need me — many times you will want me, then I shall not come; I came to open the bud so that it may blossom, not to lead your life for you."

Hearing him say this to me, I knew within my very being that he was right, that now I must prepare to make my forward journey alone… without him.

"Is it now that you are going?" I asked him.

"Not yet, you will know when…" and then he departed.

Peter had, up to this time, been bringing me bodily back to life with his healings and love — now feeling my true self, our relationship started changing. I was now aware that our marriage, however loving, needed to be on a more spiritual basis, and he agreed. Before, I would ask Peter's advice, but I now found I knew what I had to do and sometimes this was the opposite to his thinking; the change in our relationship came about slowly, but surely, with even more perfect love between us than before.

I had gone into an early meditation at two am and was just sitting on a bean bag, in my usual position, basking in the divine peace one feels after a good meditation, when I was aware of an overriding power within the room and of Sri Yukteswarji and Babaji's presence. I knew within me that they were here for a special purpose and as body and mind sat still, in the powerful peace, I felt forced to open my eyes — a light like a flickering flame, was just in front and above me, it started descending towards me; my eyes closed again and my whole being felt as though it was receiving this light, first in my head and then my whole inner self, but not in my mortal body. As this was happening, I was aware of an accolade and an awareness being made to me and within me that *this was the Holy Ghost, the Holy Spirit* that was spoken about in the Bible, the one that helped us 'speak with many tongues', — with these knowing thoughts I went into a cosmic state. Time passed and I know not how long I sat there imbibing without taking in the full awareness of the proceedings. I then became aware of one of their voices saying my names, "Mata Yogananda, you have a new name — 'Mahasaya'[17] — go with these names and start your work as a true Guru. Our pledge to you, is that your love and *WISDOM* will never desert you and will always be with you." With these words said, they departed and the room became just a room once more, with my return to a more mortal level and I sat for a long time in the divine peace that was present and sat… and sat…

The following day, I woke up without being called, as now it had become a good habit to wake early in the morning and start my day, in the only way one should, with meditation. Guruji came after my meditation to speak with me and then I told him of all yesterday's happenings and asked him what it all meant.

"You know, you do not have to ask me." He said.

But I replied, "The Holy Ghost enabled a person to speak with many tongues, I cannot." — he chuckled and said, "Many tongues means with great wisdom and insights."

Feeling a complete fool, I just had to continue, "But how do I know I am a Guru… I am still me."

His gentle comment was, "Outside, bodily, maybe not — inside *you* are; accept this title, it has been given to you as your rightful one, with your further acknowledgement of the name Mahasaya." "Oh", that took me by surprise as I had not told him of that. It was taking a long time to realize he knew *everything* there was to know about me.

"Please, help me to see my worth." I asked him, for up to now, I had felt pretty worthless.

"As this is the last time we shall meet, as we have been doing, I will tell you a little more. Your last existence was in India, where you had a family, for a while, but then your divine progress made a separation, sufficient for you to forsake that part of your life and go to help all those that crossed your path. Now, you are reborn in the West — help others find their way back to peace and love; you were born as mortal and as

Western as possible, so that people will see and hear the Master's message once more 'be like children, let the lamb lie down with the wolf' and let them prove once more that love is *All Powerful.*" He continued, saying "Now that you know these facts of your past life, you must forget them, only to remember them if you fail in your mind to remember that you are worthy of this path."

I wanted to ask him so much more, and to tell him how much I loved him and all the great Masters and Gurus, but the words could not gain exit from my mouth.

As my thoughts travelled in all directions, feeling the loss of his presence already, and wondering if I would *ever be allowed* to divulge anything about my Guru, he must have read my thoughts for he answered saying,

"You must keep these happenings to yourself, until I say otherwise to you, it is for your own good... for your protection and it will allow you to centre your work without any problems, that would undoubtedly be presented to you, if these happenings between us were made known...

"You must teach the meditation and the truths that have been taught you, keeping the essences, but putting it into a more acceptable style for Western people who have little time to spare, yet desire to reach Self–Realization in this lifetime."

"This is a great responsibility." I retorted.

"Indeed, and one that you need not take on, unless you wish to." How gentle and wise he was with me, but I knew only too well that come what may — whatever the consequences, I would take up and do anything that was asked of me by my Guru, or Gurus, for if I could help, even in a small way, people to find peace and love, then this I knew, in my 'heart of hearts', was now the most important thing in my life for me to do... and I said so. We sat quietly.

"My blessings and love are with you — remember that I shall be nearer to you than I have ever been before." I knew he was telling me that 'we were at one'[18] with the Divine Love prevailing over all.

With these last words, he left me feeling very sad, but also with a renewed vigour to get on with the next

STEP IN MY LIFE.

Do Your Best
for
This is all that is asked
of you

33

Going to America

ALTHOUGH, inwardly, I felt it was the right time to go to America, somehow confirmation was needed, by an outward sign. "It's an enormous amount of money to find and a long way to go, please may I see the face of Daya Mata giving me her blessing". This was said as I sat gazing at some flowers on a mantelpiece, in one of our healing rooms.

"I will sit here until some confirmation comes." I said, and it did.

After a good half hour, feeling dejected and uncertain of my trip abroad, I suddenly beheld Daya Mata sitting in a lotus position, with hands upraised, gently together, giving me her blessing; a gentle soft smile tinged her face and then she was gone from my mortal sight.

My confirmation for the journey had been given to me; it may be wondered, why I did not ask to see Paramahansaji, my Guru, or Babaji, but as all Gurus are Self/God realized... if true ones, then it stands to reason that they *are all as one,* in love for all. There is no separation... you pray to one — all will hear... and as they are at one with life... the Universe... God — so there is *only unity of all, everywhere.*

Such is the knowledge of true Self–Realization — so to me, my love for Daya Mata is as for all souls... the *same.*

After giving my profound thanks for the confirmation that I had to get to America, as soon as possible, my prayers went out for help as I started constructively looking into every possible way of finding the fare, and a companion to go with me... .

I woke up one morning, knowing that it was time for me to make plans to go to America.

"Peter, I am going to America, soon." I said.

"With what?" Peter asked, "We have no money, at least not enough to do that."

I could not be shaken from my enthusiasm, "If it is meant to happen, and it will happen, because Guruji said so, then I will get the money," I replied.

I knew I had to go, not only to talk to people, but to visit Paramahansaji's Ashrams. The whole reason why, was not known to me... yet.

Someone, a person more knowledgeable about these matters than myself, said to me, "Oh, you will need to hire a car over there."

In my naivety I replied, "No, I'll hop on a bus." *That* was what I thought, and of course was proved wrong.

I asked Tina if she would like to come with me... when the money arrived, "Yes, I would." She said, "Will we have time to go to Hollywood and perhaps Disneyland?"

"I hope so," I replied, "We will need a fortnight though to do it all."

A little later, our friend Bill, hearing of my plans said he had a lot of dollars over from his last trip abroad and would I like a loan of them. This, I knew, was the news that I had been waiting for. We now had the money; the tickets were found at low cost by a friend of Linda's and off we went to the American Embassy in London, to get our visas and soon we were on our way with an address in Los Angeles, where we hoped to find reasonable lodgings.

Our plane journey was uneventful; Tina had travelled abroad many times before, so she knew all the 'ins and outs' of travelling. Knowing this, I left it all in her capable hands. Tina has such a wonderful sense of humour and is a very easy going person, so to have her with me was a great joy; only one thing blighted it and that was, she was not herself; in fact she was not at all well during the whole of the fortnight — it transpired, on our return to England, that she had a virus, no wonder she had been tired and fretful.

On arrival at Los Angeles airport, we retrieved our luggage and took a cab to downtown LA. On finding the said address, and trying others as well, we decided it was not too bad for the price; a large room with two five foot beds and bathroom, en suite, awaited us.

I cannot truthfully tell the order of events from here, as so much happened; I will simply write as the pen moves me.

On seeing the distances that we had to travel, we hired a car, a sports model that I had not driven before; the man who hired it to us gave me the keys and left me to it. A few lights switched on and off... windscreen wipers going... later... I pressed the right buttons and started off on our journey. I seemed to manage to manoeuvre the car on the roads quite well, but when it came to roundabouts... the car never seemed to go around the correct way! Do you know what it is like, in England, let alone downtown Los Angeles having people blow their horns at you nonstop?!

The sky was blue and cloudless, the sun shone, warming our bodies and making us feel welcome as we drove to Disneyland. Tina nearly got arrested — her hair colour... this time it was purple-red. Separated from me by her speed of walking, she was approached by a policeman who wanted to ask her some questions — on seeing me, he apologised for his intrusion and went his way.

I had come to America with the only clothes that I had that I thought would be suitable; unfortunately, they were only suitable for helping Tina with such problems as those described above! I could have done with a lesson, or two, on how to dress in the sun on a low budget. On getting into Disneyland, being both young at heart, we thoroughly enjoyed ourselves; the same when we went to see Hollywood and its film makers. We clapped and laughed at the stunt men until our ribs ached... we were children... enjoying ourselves.

We had been to several of the different churches in Los Angeles, and now we were to visit the Ashrams of the Self-Realization

Fellowship. I had waited a long time for this moment, now it was here, I drove with apprehension towards the Hollywood Fellowship Temple. The Temple itself was temporarily closed, which saddened me, for to meditate in all the Ashrams had been my desire; it was not to be.

"Come on Tina, let's go to the bookshop," I said, having seen it placed off the main road, a little further up from where we were. There were so many things I wanted to do; I wanted to meditate and see all the Brothers and Sisters that I could and ply them with questions. We entered the bookshop to find a good many books, but an unsmiling face — one that did not even look up on my saying hello. How could this be with one of the S.R.F. Sisters, I felt unwanted, and turned away pondering on what was going on inside her to make her look like she did.

The following day I said to Tina, "I want very much to visit the Mother Centre in Los Angeles, will you come? I might get lost if you don't." I added laughingly.

"Yes, I will," said Tina, "But will you be long?"

"No, not very long." I replied.

I had by then already tried to make an appointment with Daya Mata, but as she was away at the time, I said I would like to see Brother Achalananda, if possible — it was, so we set off early in the afternoon for my appointment at 2.30pm, plenty of time, in normal circumstances! Understandably, we lost ourselves and it was not until 3.30pm that we entered the grounds of the Mother Centre, both feeling bedraggled and tired; Tina said she would wait outside for me. I was by no means ready to meet Brother Achalananda — my cotton skirt was all creased, my top clung to me with perspiration caused by the heat of the day and my lamentably late arrival!

I walked into a large entrance hall in which the silence that reigned there was peaceful; they were preparing for Kriya Yoga initiations, so I could not sit in the Chapel, or see it. I made my humble apologies to a most serene looking Sister sitting at a desk and asked to see Brother Achalananda, "Oh, you must mean Brother Anandamoy," she said.

"No," I replied, knowing full well that he was the one people usually see, "I want to see Brother Achalananda." Why I asked to see him I did not know, and I was made to ask for him a second time — to ask only for him; he was the only man I was being allowed to think of at that time. A few minutes elapsed before I saw him coming towards me; we shook hands and sat down. He asked me what my connection was with Yoganandaji; and I truthfully told him my story.

I could see that he was becoming very agitated with what I was saying and he told me it could not have happened and that it was easy to believe things that are not so. "We have been warned about people saying these things," he said, "Guruji would not teach anyone outside this S.R.F." He asked me then, "Have you read the lessons in our written courses?"

"No," I replied, "I have been taught these verbally and certainly, all I need to know." He did not answer this, and while waiting, I sent a fervent prayer to Guruji to help us. Brother Achalananda was a kind man from what I saw of him, but up to date all he had done was try to persuade me that Yoganandaji was limited — this I could not believe. No Guru is ever limited or tied down in transport of themselves. He repeated all of Guruji's sayings, but used none of his own.

I prayed and waited.

"You know," the brother said, "I was once talking to someone like yourself who was very advanced, but still they read my lessons." Now his face had changed, his voice was quite Indian and he couldn't help but gulp occasionally. I knew these signs well, Guruji was using his voice to speak to me; I bowed to him and listened. He asked me to accept the lessons and enrol while I was there, that I must read them all, they would be needed in the future. After saying this and going on to speak further to me of things of a personal nature, he then finished. The utter surprise on the Brother's face, was a wonder to behold, but it was sad to think he could not have used his natural powers to decide the truth of the matter. No word was said; he bowed to me and I to him before he left me.

The soul sitting at the desk was love personified, so caring, so gentle; she gave me a form to fill in and asking for no money, said I would receive the lessons, in due course. We spoke... without speaking. Her light was radiant.

I went out to sit under a tree in meditation and to look at the famed cacti without thorns, which was written about in Guruji's book. The sister who would have shown me around, was restless, waiting for relatives, I believe, so I asked to be left to show myself around. I found the tree where Guruji used to sit with devotees and his presence comforted me. I wanted to sit and think, but Tina was restless to go; she looked white and drawn, so we departed. It was now evening and dark and we lost our way, only to find it again but returned to our room very late.

I had so much to think about, now that I had been to the Mother Centre, but — a feeling came within me, not to even try to sort it out until I returned to England.

We decided to move to the coast to get some sea–air; I thought this might help Tina, as well as myself. I knew that everything would be all right and that there was a reason for all these happenings, even Tina not being well; I was being sorely tried on many counts. My knowledge that the 'whys and wherefores' would show themselves in due course, and that I was here to learn, as well as do something important, kept me on course.

We found a room just over the road, by the sea, in Santa Monica. We talked, walked, and rested; our meals consisted of a good breakfast, a milk shake... like only the Americans can make, at lunchtime and then, in the evening a meal in a restaurant of a different nationality each night, for our last meal of the day; this way we were able to balance our money without using our plastic cards.

One day, while walking on the sand, Tina was telling me that she did not know how her life would turn out and that she had many problems that were worrying her. We sat down on the sand and I made a drawing, in the sand, from which I told her some of her future. I could have told her without the sand, but she would not have believed me — I thought that this way she might, and thereby it would help her, to a degree.

It is only when true need is shown and with permission, will I tell anyone of future events — it would be wrong otherwise and would harm them more than help them; knowing the responsibility that one has, when one is given the ability to do this, I do not misuse the privilege.

One day I suggested that we make a journey out to another S.R.F. Centre called 'Lake Shrine', Pacific Palisades; taking my 'map reader' with me, we set off along the Freeway. Tina's map reading was excellent and we arrived there with plenty of daylight to spare. This was a beautiful retreat — the beauty and peace gave off celestial music and light; I dearly wanted to stop and meditate for a while, so we sat down in the Boat House by the lake. I was aware of a Brother staring in our direction and I felt hostility and the need to move on. Tina had taken a photograph by the lake and later, on leaving the Shrine, I saw a notice forbidding people to take photographs — why didn't the Brother tell us? As it happened, the photographs did not print, when we tried to have them developed, so all was well.

Once more, on our arrival here, we found the Temple closed for repair work, though this time we did look inside. We bought tapes and books from the Indian shop and then it was time to go; I had asked if there were any Brothers we could meet, as we had come a long way... from England, but they were busy at the time and hence, no one was available.

We were into our second week by now and Tina said she would like to see the San Diego Zoo, which we did; it was a confining Zoo for the animals, we were not at all impressed and left soon after arriving.

The following day, Tina suggested that we went to San Francisco; I agreed, thinking it was just around the corner, as it were! Finding it would be a long journey of many hours, I asked her if she would like to come to Encinitas with me — "Where is that?" Tina asked. "Well," I said, "It is not as far as San Francisco." — and off we went.

The weather had become very hot now, with the sun beating down on us as we drove along the many laned freeway, cars either side of us. I felt very vulnerable and wondered what on earth I was doing, musing that it would be much safer on a racetrack. We arrived at the Ashram in Encinitas only to find there were no rooms available that night and Paramahansaji's room was out of bounds due to it being decorated, but it would be available in a few days time. The Sister said it would be possible to be shown around the Ashram and she very kindly gave us an address to try for Bed and Breakfast, and told us there would be a service in the chapel that night, if we wished to attend. I thanked her and then proceeded to look around the gardens of the Ashram that led to the sea. Once more, the deep longing to meditate came upon me, but Tina reminded me that we had not found anywhere to stay yet, the day was nearly over and she was tired, so we took ourselves off to search; we were fortunate to find accommodation nearby, next door to the S.R.F. Temple.

That evening, while Tina retired early, I quickly changed and went with haste, to the chapel. The Temple was small, but beautiful; the people assembling there looked like devotees from the Ashram and they filled the temple. I sat in a front pew, near the altar, so that I could retreat into myself. A brother came in and gave us a talk, then a prayer was said and finally, the brother led us all in singing *"I am the bubble, make me the sea"* — a very beautiful chant. At last, I had a chance to commune and meditate — I felt Guruji's presence, then I entered a blissful state, I was lost to everything going on around me, yet I knew of its existence. My joy, my peace... my bliss, at last I could stay and be as one — my hunger was being satisfied... my thirst quenched.

When the service was over, I stayed, while I was aware of the devotees disbanding. On leaving, the brother looked enquiringly at me, but I could do no more than nod.

O blissful Samadhi.

The next day, we headed towards the sea, where we sat and watched the surfers enjoying themselves. It was interesting to see there was a policeman on hand, checking to see that no one was drinking any alcohol — how sensible.

Midday came, and I felt it was time to start our journey back to Santa Monica; my feeling was to keep going and not stop off for food. This proved very wise, for on our return, as the car gently pulled in at the Motel, the engine stopped completely — next day, they came for the car.

One more day walking and watching some of the youngsters jog down the palm leafed tracks by the sea; others were sitting in a meditative state, while one or two were practising Asanas, or Shiatsu. All these youngsters were respectably dressed for the occasion — they were not flaunting their bodies in any way whatsoever. Unfortunately, in England, this is not always so; no shyness, no embarrassment, just enjoyment. Perhaps my view, because of my short stay, was a little 'rosy', but I liked what I saw of the people around me.

Good bye America.

34

Back Home

*D*URING this time at Ansford, we had patients coming to us, as a result of the group discussion we had some time ago, when we invited other professional people, to meet us. One such person who came, was a Peter Casley, the Rev. Casley's son. He had been in a motor cycle accident — whilst driving his bike one day, he was pushed over by a passing lorry. Since then, he had suffered pains in his body and had been left with a ringing noise continually in his ears. "Could you do anything for me?" he asked. We explained that we could, but that we would prefer to give him a healing first, and from that, we could find out about his condition, then we would have another talk.

After explaining the healing to him, we asked him to lie on the couch, then placed a light covering over him, with his shoes and glasses off; he looked very relaxed. After completing his treatment, on the couch and then on the stool, we could tell him, with all honesty, that a lot could be done for him, if he would trust us and take our advice. He did all these things, and over the weeks, became well again with no noise in the ears, and a painless body. As he thanked us both and proceeded to walk out of the door and down the stairs, I said to Peter, "He is for me", which was a phrase I was to use many times in the future.

"What do you mean by that?" asked Peter.

"I do not know exactly," was my reply, "But he was meant to come here and meet us and soon I will have much to teach him." Having said this, it soon went out of my mind.

The stairs that led up to our flat where we had the two healing rooms, were steep stairs, and were about fifteen in number; we never enquired if people might not be able to climb them; there was only one man in all our time there who we had to help upstairs. We found that people with heart problems improved with the exercise and several of these would call on us and tell us they felt the stairs were therapy for them.

We now had animals being brought to us by their owners, and we kept a special blanket for this purpose, with water bowl and towel to hand. There were mainly dogs and cats at that time, and as numbers increased, we wondered about starting a separate day, solely for animals, but it never seemed to work out for the best that way.

We were now adding lectures to our list of activities, which we would hold in the downstairs room; we had a good attendance, with one or two people coming to 'heckle' us — this brought back memories of such people in Hyde Park and I felt quite able to deal with them. In fact, I would turn it to our advantage and this gave many an evening an added 'zest' for all those present; we got to know the ones like Miss Piers, who did not come to learn. Peter Casley would come to all of them and would help us beforehand, with chairs and the tea preparations, which we valued greatly. We got to know Pauline and Jim Allen, who lived nearby, very well and they were very supportive to us; she was not only broad-minded, with strong view points, but would stand up for all that she believed in when confronted with her beliefs. From Pauline, we found our first cleaning lady, called Jane, who also cleaned house for the Allens. She was someone we trusted implicitly and she took responsibility for keeping the Centre clean and tidy. What a boon and a friend she was to us; I might add, she kept us in order as well!

By now, we were getting tired of going down the stairs of one flat, and up the other to the healing rooms, so we had a door put in our bedroom through to the healing room and then hung a velvet curtain over the door, to hide it. Len, who with his wife Iris had leased the flat before us, became our friends and it was he who put a lovely old door in place for us; he had stripped and stained it — it was one of the old–fashioned arched garden doors, the wood being of oak and its thickness made it a thing of beauty. I was sad to have to leave it behind, when we moved from there.

Sometimes, when a patient was sitting with their eyes closed, relaxing, before leaving, I would need something that I had left in our flat. On opening the oak door quietly, I would go through to retrieve the wanted article. The patient, unknown to me, had opened their eyes and not seeing me there, closed them again; their surprise on opening them once more to see me sitting there was amusing — perhaps they thought I was another 'Paul Daniels'[19] . Only one patient ever asked us what was behind the curtain.

We made many friends of our patients, after we had treated them; a Mr. and Mrs. Beunk, who came to England from South Africa and a Mr. and Mrs. Pratt, also from South Africa, but they had lived in England for some time. These people, most in fact, came in trepidation, to see what we were like and more importantly, to find out if we could help them. We now had a committee of six people, formed especially to promote new ideas for the Centre. From one idea put forward, we started a jumble sale, which we called 'Rags to Riches'; we decided to hold this annually. What a task it was; exhausting, but interesting. We first held it in our downstairs room, but soon moved it to the local Methodist Hall. This became a well attended event, but because we kept the best of the jumble that was left each year, until the next, it grew in piles of books and bric–a–brac, until it almost took up a complete room. We decided that we needed the room more than the jumble, so we stopped holding them.

Every jumble sale must have its 'petite thieves' and so we did. It was interesting, I would spot them and watch them stuff items into their bags, but instead of saying anything to them, I worked on the basis that they must need those items more than we did, so I would look at them, acknowledging to them that I knew what they had done, and leave it to their consciences. I know at least one such person who stopped doing this because of the acknowledging, without the threatening behaviour that was usually given to them.

I remember, when I was three or four years of age, finding that I could stand on a chair and get a chocolate biscuit out of the cupboard. Soon, I had demolished quite a few, but mother, on catching me out... did not smack me... she just said "Judy, I did not think you would do that, you have hurt me — I trusted you". Even at that tender age, it taught me a lesson I have not forgotten.

Our life was soon to change.

Mrs Hiscock needed her ground back; it was now a lovely patio and vegetable patch. We had laid the patio with coloured slabs and had a hammock which swung with the breeze and looked onto a small rockery and then a glory of flowers. The vegetable garden was producing large, beautiful vegetables and was our creation and joy. But it *had* to go... and sad we were.

Next we were informed that the Inn would have to be sold. Would we like to buy it? This was impossible, as we did not have a bank balance of that proportion and it was always our belief not to hoard money, but to keep it in circulation, to a sensible degree. Let us keep positive I said and pray — if we are meant to stay in Somerset, then we shall be shown the way. Peter agreed and we kept the stillness within... waiting for an answer to our dilemma. Our patients were told that we may not be in Ansford for long, but they still came. One afternoon, Bill Beunk came for his treatment and informed us that he might be able to help us. His wife, Dee and himself had been left some money and he wondered if we would accept a house on a rental basis, if they found one in Castle Cary; and if we did, would we say it was a consortium who owned it, if we were asked about it, as they wished to stay incognito. Dee was also keen on this idea, and we said yes, we would love to stay in Castle Cary, if the premises felt right for us.

In fact, the premises they found were ideal; and Bill being very good with his hands, helped turn the premises into a good working

Centre. The building was in Station Road, Castle Cary; it consisted of four rooms downstairs, kitchen and outside toilet. Upstairs were three rooms and a bathroom with a toilet, plus a very large garage, an outhouse to the side with a garden border and a carport.

By the time Bill had finished with the premises, we had three healing rooms downstairs, a small waiting room and office with a small room for healing animals, and the toilet became enclosed. The three rooms upstairs became bedrooms; one en suite, which we had. The garage became one large room with special wall panelling and a sprung floor, which I was to use for dance therapy and as a lecture room, it could be divided into two rooms if necessary. Bill had built a further floor over the garage consisting of a Meditation room and sitting room, while making the outhouse into a kitchen, with a partly open storehouse. This was to be ours, on a rental basis. First, we had to play our part and decorate the rooms, which we did with local help, but the carpet laying was purely ours to do. Cutting up good Wilton and Axminster carpet, binding and gluing it, is in my mind, one of the hardest jobs to do in a house. When we had completed this, my neck and back were in trouble again, but *I now knew* how to control pain, so I did not feel it — there was no time to spare for my body just now. We had taken the carpets from our living quarters, so that we could still see our patients in a fully furnished healing room; this meant combining healing and moving, together, so that by the time we had a healing room ready in our new Centre, we could take patients there while completing the rest of the move.

The day came for our move with a borrowed truck and several friends.

*We are all
One*

35

We Move Yet Again

S O our practice grew, and we got to know Dee and Bill very well, as their house was next door to us, in fact, they had a garden gate that led into our side entrance. Their two Jack Russells, Charka and Gemmy soon became very dear to us; Charka would wait for us to open the gate in the morning and bark loudly to tell us he was *there*. When Charka arrived, I knew we had a special relationship that transcended this life, and so it has remained.

One day, Dee and Bill asked us if we would like to live in their house and be caretakers of it for them; we could then use the other rooms in the Centre for visitors and patients. We were thrilled with the idea as we were already turning away people who wanted to come and stay at the Centre.

It was agreed that we would always keep a room ready for them whenever they wanted to come and stay... for now they wanted to travel abroad more and would only be home occasionally. We had Charka and Gemmy and they became like our own.

*We need
Spiritual Knowledge
To set us free*

36

Getting to Know the Media

"PETE Murray wants us to go on his phone–in radio programme," Peter informed me, after we had finished one day. "When is this?" I asked. "Next week" Peter said, "At 11pm in London, but we need to be there at 10.30pm."

We took the car up and travelled back in the early hours of the morning, ready for healing the following day. Peter Murray was one of the Radio's early Disc Jockeys who I had photographed and had also printed hundreds of photos, for his fans; this was when I was at Lee Israel's — so I knew him. He did not remember me, and why should he, but he is a kind man whom I believe helps an enormous amount of people, in many different ways. He made the broadcast very easy for us and we enjoyed the whole experience.

A few months later, we saw an article in the local daily newspaper about ourselves and learnt that a patient had written in to them about our animal healing work. Soon after that, we had *The Observer, Daily Mirror* and other papers, contact us — would we give them an interview? We said yes to *The Observer* and in the same week a reporter and photographer arrived to see us. The 'splash' in *The Observer* brought us hundreds of letters and telephone calls which needed a secretary to deal with them; we had not got one, so we made do with ourselves.

Following on from these happenings, we then had *ITV South West* contact us — we are interested in your animal healing, they told us. "How did you hear about us?" I asked them —

"The Observer article," was the reply; they wanted to do a programme with us healing animals and they wanted to meet the owners — "Can that be arranged?" they asked. I said "Yes, but can you give me a week to set it all up?" They said they had no objection to this request. I hurriedly rang around for cats, dogs, parrots and owners who would not mind being filmed, for not everyone, including myself, likes the limelight. This was all arranged and organised, to the best of my ability and filming took place the following morning, and lasted all day. I never realised how much *fine* organisation the whole project needed, for that is what it was.

The film crew were an exceptionally nice group of men; the people who brought their animals along to the Centre had the patience of *Job,* and the animals were wonderful.

The television station wanted not only small animals, but also large and unusual ones; unfortunately, though we could have found a horse or two, we could not have got them through the front door, but we had a large dog who had difficulty walking and standing up — he was shown on TV jumping off the couch — we could not stop him! An introvert parrot, who would not go to anyone, except its owner, flew on to our shoulders and after the healing, returned to its owner; cats that purred and a Guinea Pig that liked 'doggy' company and sat between their paws, taking notice.

By the end of the day, with arc lights that had been fully upon us, many interviews, healings and numerous keeping of cats from dogs, we retired, thinking that perhaps actors and actresses *do* earn all the money that they get.

When this was televised, we were inundated with phone calls and letters, once again. It was hard work and we put in long hours, but we did enjoy it and were pleased that animal healing was getting recognition at last.

Shortly after this episode, Peter Casley came back into our lives more prominently.

"Can I work here, with you?" asked Peter.

"What do you want to work at?" I asked him.

"Well, I am not certain," he said, "My feeling is to do anything you want me to and that way I should find out".

Peter Casley was working in a local shoe shop; he wanted a change. He had already arranged an appointment with another firm with a view to taking a different job, but said he would not go for this interview, if we wanted him. On telling me this, I asked him to come back, that is, if he wanted to, *after* he had been for this other interview. This he did, only to say he would like to join us... I knew from what he said that he had been offered over one hundred pounds a week when he went for the other interview — with us it could only be ten pounds, though he could live in with us if he wished, as there was a smaller room at the Centre that he could have, and eat with us when he felt like it.

"You would be on reception to begin with." I told him.

"I would like that." He replied.

"Have you ever done any reception work?" I asked.

"No," he replied, "But I am willing to learn."

The gentleness, shyness, but firmness in his reply, plus all his help in the past, made me say, "We would like you here with us, but what about the money, it is not very much for you."

"I can manage, thank you." He said "I would like to work here and will think about the accommodation." His mother and father were moving, soon, to Cornwall and he wondered whether to go with them, but decided not to, and chose to be part of our family.

Peter Casley worked as receptionist and did any other work that came along — he was always eager to learn. One day I said to him "Peter, your name should really be Daniel now." He just said "Do you think so?" Slowly, but surely, he started to like the name Daniel and rebuked me if I called him Peter, so now we had a Daniel.

There was a rapport between Daniel and myself that grew deeper with time, and though few words of affection were spoken, the love was there. We would spend many hours in the evenings — him asking me questions on any topic, my answering. We covered everything there was to cover. Meanwhile, I asked him if he would like to be a healer, he did not jump at it, but we knew he would be an excellent one, so we taught him and asked him to sit in on all our lectures and courses, if he wished to... he did.

One day, I asked him if he had thought about a Guru, "What is that?" he asked me. I explained at length and went on to say, "You know I am your Guru, if you want me". He wanted to believe what I said, but found it difficult. "I am here if you need me," was all I said and we continued with his training.

When the time was right for him, he asked me to teach and guide him in Meditation and the bond then developed between us as Guru and disciple, and he grew in stature, as *DANIEL*.

Peter and myself were married by this time, with a slip of paper to prove it, but in my own eyes, it was not the true marriage ceremony — that had taken place in God's eyes, a long time ago.

"Rena, the *BBC TV* people want to speak to someone about making a programme on healing." Daniel informed me.

"Shall I take it?" I asked, taking the phone from his hand. "Can I help you?" I asked.

"We would like to come and film you healing animals," they said, "And we would also like to hear the owners side of how they feel about their animals and them having healing."

"Fine." I said, but remembering the last time we were filmed with the same procedure, I suggested that it be left for ten days or more.

"Not possible," they said, "We want it for next week."

Well, I thought, why not?! Once more, but with Daniel helping us this time, we had another day's filming. From this showing on 'prime time' we were inundated, once more, with letters and phone calls. Since then, animal healing has become well known, but then it was 'new' news, hence the notice taken of us.

We had also been invited to go on *Channel 4* to talk about healing with the resident vet; this we did. He did not take to us and I cannot say I was enthralled with him, but we tried to find a talking point with him, till we realised that he had no intention of having a friendly discussion and I believe he was out for our 'blood'. Knowing this brought out the competitive spirit in me, and a lively

The Mother and Father of Mata Yogananda

Their house in
Wedderburn Road
Hampstead
London, NW3

Mata Yogananda at her confirmation
into the Catholic faith

Mata Yogananda after her return from France, 1953

Mata
Yogananda's
three
daughters

Mata
Yogananda
at the beach,
June 1973

Four
generations
of Dentons.
Albert Denton
on the right,
with Peter as a
small boy

The Old Ansford Inn (above and below) – Mata Yogananda and
Peter Sevananda's first healing centre in Somerset.
The scene of Mata Yogananda's intensive training with her Guru.

Paramahansa Yogananda; Mata Yogananda's Guru

Masters

Ji Jesus

Swami Sri
Yukteswarji

Babaji

Lahiri Mahasayaji

Mata Yogananda and Peter Sevananda (above)
at the Centre in Castle Cary, Somerset (below)

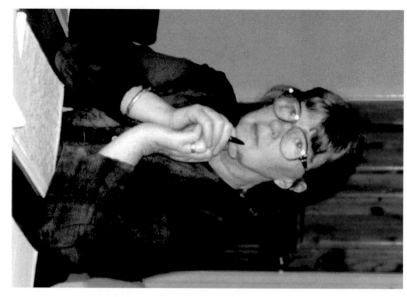

Mata Yogananda and Peter Sevananda at work on this book.

Harold
and
Joyce
Pratt

Mata Yogananda with some of the family
in the Mother Centre gardens

Main House of the Self Realization Meditation Healing Centre (Mother Centre) in Queen Camel, Somerset. Home of the Alpha—Omega Family.

Mata Yogananda and Peter Sevananda
with Charka and Sammy in the Mother Centre Garden (above)

Mother Centre family at work (above)

Inside the
Small Meditation
Room at the
Mother Centre.

The Yogananda Room at the Mother Centre (above)

Inside the Yogananda Room (above)
(readers note: SRMHC Meditation Stools, designed under Mata Yogananda's guidance ~ for all people who wish to have one, visible in this picture.)

Part of the extensive gardens of the Mother Centre

The Lodge
(above) and
Owl Cottage (left),
some of the
Mother Centre's
accommodations where
people stay when they
come for peace and
healing.

Daoseva (above)
The Garden of Serenity (below) ~
the Mother Centre's *Oriental*-themed Garden

A guest chalet (above)
and swimming pool (below)

Mata Yogananda at the Mother Centre

At Mata Yogananda's Cave of Silence

The Self Realization Meditation Healing Centre,
Christchurch, New Zealand (above)

The Christchurch Centre family (above)

The Self Realization Meditation Healing Centre,
Halfmoon Bay, British Columbia, Canada (above)

The Self Realization Meditation Healing Centre,
Bath, Michigan, USA (above)

Mata Yogananda Mahasaya Dharma

The Self Realization Meditation Healing Centre,
Auckland, New Zealand

exchange took place. We were not trying to, but I am not ashamed to say, we got the better of this situation and conversation, so much so, it is sad to say they cut it out of the programme, leaving nothing, in my humble opinion, of any vital interest to the viewers. I know truth is sometimes unpalatable, but the day it is listened to will be a very important one.

We were well and truly settled by now in the Centre and the house; Daniel worked well with us and became one of the family — we became a good working unit. It is true to say that Daniel had a lot to learn and he did not find the first few months very easy, until the day came when he stopped fighting life and himself, accepting his path and willingly going in faith… that day he grew greatly and has not looked back in his spiritual progress since.

Questions abounded from him.

One of his most difficult thoughts to overcome was *WISDOM IS ALWAYS RIGHT* — the fact that it came from me, a woman, *his Guru,* who was not dressed in long flowing robes, who cooked, cleaned and was not continually in meditation, proved difficult for him to accept. I saw his dilemma, but all I could do was to wait patiently for him to see the light of truth. After all, he had been brought up in the Methodist faith, my words were foreign to his ears and, as he experienced life within the Centre, he also experienced life out of the Centre. Finally, having passed all the tests that he had given me knowingly, and unknowingly, he then gave me his love and devotion.

I had been giving lectures and talks, with and without Peter, for a while now; the Women's Institute, professional bodies and schools, were an outlet for these. The varying courses in Meditation, Healing and Dance Therapy were full. The Dance Therapy Course consisted of using spiritual psychology and body movements to help the person towards wholeness; this was an in–depth healing in itself. I quickly realised that in everyday healings, dance, posture and breathing advice could be given, if needed. On this basis, I therefore discontinued the dance therapy course, and put in the 'Way of Life' for children, a course that became very popular.

I am
You are
We are
God

37

Devon ~ Dartmoor

OUR few days at Dartmoor were very pleasant.
    We had come for a quick 'recharge', both being very tired and knowing there was more work to go back to. We went purely on our feelings and the need, certainly not on the 'wanting' aspect — any occasion that we were away was always very special… with the accommodation, area and climate being exactly what we needed for that moment of time.

Anyone can work on this basis, if they wish — the only requirement is to cut out the 'I want' and put in its place *is it a need?* — *do I need it… now?* If you diverge from this knowledge and principle, it will get you into trouble.

For example… one morning, we were going shopping, the shops were just over a mile away. I was feeling very tired and it was a cold day, but I went to put on my boots and had a strong feeling, not to do so. This feeling presided within me, but I shook it off… put them on, and set off down the road, to buy food for the next few days that we were to be there. No sooner had we started down the slope, than I slipped; thinking nothing of this, I proceeded on, only to slip again. Still not listening to the wisdom of my feelings, I was nearly at the shops when I sprained my ankle.

It was extremely painful.

Peter said, "What do you feel you should do?" I smiled, I knew what I should have done… but too late.

"Wait just a few minutes," was my reply, "while I put into practice that which I had learnt from Rydal. 'Ask and you will receive'."

"Dear Infinite Beloved," I said, "Help me get to the shops and home. I ask your forgiveness and will try never to disobey again". Humbly, I said these words and instantaneously, I started walking as though nothing was the matter with me, with no pain whatever, in my ankle; I virtually marched to the shops and back.

My walking back, though uphill, was at a faster pace than Peter's, he even had difficulty keeping up with me. My arms were swinging, my feet marching and my body and head were erect. What an experience; just as we reached the door of our flatlet, I was in pain again and had to rest.

This reminds me of a time I was in the car driving home, after a very tiring day; my back was hurting and I was finding it difficult to change gear. The steering wheel was actually taken out of my control and being manipulated! Not only that, but also the brakes. I was in awe, but kept a clear mind and let it happen, knowing all was well. I tried once to change gear and found I could not — I did this just to see how bad my back was.

On arriving home, I gave thanks to *whomever.*

I might add to this story that I tried to get this to happen once when *I did not need the help* and nearly came to an untimely end.

A SINNER STILL.

38

Reflections on America ~ Los Angeles

MY journey to Los Angeles, California, in America, had left me contemplating its reasons and the advantages of my having needed to go. What had I learnt? What did Guruji expect me to see and learn, was more to the point. As my thoughts lingered on this subject, a door seemed to open within, allowing me to have clear vision of all that had taken place, and the importance of it all was shown to me, in a sequence of shots in animated light, like in a slide projection, projecting each slide long enough to be able to take in the whole picture, only with it, came the answers to all the unanswered questions that I had desperately wanted to ask before going on this pilgrimage journey.

The travelling had certainly brought a 'bubble' back into my life, and the knowledge that I was still capable of travelling and driving a car abroad, gave me back any confidence that I may have lost.

The joys and the problems that Tina and myself shared — travelling, finding adequate accommodation and sharing what little money we had, we shared these as friends more than as mother and daughter and these memories are to be treasured. Our visiting of the churches and ashrams enabled me to see more clearly the problems that larger groups and organisations had; how the grounds at all the ashrams were laid out, their buildings, the chapels and the services — at least those that I got to, were all of interest.

My being unable to meditate in the ashrams, when I wanted to, taught me more patience and that it is not always possible to do what one wants; sometimes it is more productive, as it was that time, to meet the people, the brothers and sisters that were there, and to feel and take stock of all that was seen.

I had thought in my own limited human way, that ashrams would be different to convents and monasteries, but in fact this is not the case at all, they are very similar with regards to their rules, allocation of work and their eating and prayer times. My expectations were that all people in such places would be of a gentle, loving, non–judgemental nature; unfortunately, I met many who were not like this, on first appearance. I realised how difficult it must be for them, at times, till they overcome their 'Ego'. My seeing this made me realise more fully the difficulties involved in trying to get a spiritual family together, see them merge and become as one with unconditional love as their weapon in life, yet still maintain a degree of individuality... for it is so easy to lead a flock to water, but to make each one a responsible individual to themselves and to others... I knew this would be a different matter.

Having written this, so far, I must add that the ones that stood out with love and peace in their faces were very beautiful people indeed.

The brother that I met at the Mother House was a gentle man and I believe when Guruji spoke through him... to me, a lesson was learnt. For myself... I had, to that date, not wanted the S.R.F. lessons; after all, I had been taught them *first hand,* but I also knew that Guruji wished me to have them now, to re–digest, and also because some people would believe me more if they knew I had read them, than if I had been allowed to explain my tuition on a personal level with Yoganandaji.

To carry my meditative peace always within me was a worthy lesson, from this I knew that there would be little time for me, in the future, to indulge in long meditations. I had to carry it and myself into this world and be in it… but not of it.

Each day brought new lessons — and a strengthening up with them. Now, seeing clearly that I had to work from the very beginning, on my own, using the divine intuitiveness within me, I knew I could not copy other peoples thoughts and ways.

I finished thinking… *What a lesson!*

39

People and Events

*E*ACH year, we had an open day, when we showed people around the Centre, and answered their questions; a buffet of sandwiches and cakes would be laid out, to be enjoyed.

These were important days for the Centre. The people who were normally shy of approaching us or knocking on our door, would feel more free to come and meet us, and find out for themselves that we did not possess 'horns' and were not devils, but simply, ordinary people. They would confess their thoughts and unburden themselves and they would leave as friends, with a peace about their person. On such days as these, we would also get the people who tried to degrade us by arguing and using abusive words, with which they eventually degrade themselves. My deep caring for these people prevented me from seeing or feeling the destructive force that I know was emanating from them.

What karma they were storing up for themselves; what untold harm they were creating for themselves in mind, body and spirit. Quite often, it is the strict churchgoer, that feels anger at healing, they feel healing should only be given in the church.

A blessing is vastly different from healing, although it has untold power in it. Did not Ji Jesus and the great Saints give healings outside the church? Is their God different from anyone else's — is God's light confined only to churches and only people within the church? No, *we* will not find 'the Way', unless we stop criticism rising within.

Be as little children — how quickly they love, forgive and have *FAITH.*

People

Dee and Bill were coming home from abroad regularly now; we were becoming good friends. Life had brought us up in different lands, so our outlook on money, people, our beliefs and feelings were vastly different; consequently, there were times we would have a clash of personalities. South Africa, where they both came from, is a hard place to grow up in and still maintain a sensitive nature, due to their ethnic problems; likewise Britain's 'reasoning' had its own problems. Words, feelings and even humour are so vastly different in each land.

To understand someone, you have to understand yourself first and foremost, then *know...* and allow for other people's words, thoughts and upbringing. Taking these altogether, and adding a wish to understand them, can make a friendship blossom, as it did with myself, Bill, Dee and Peter. I believe that in each given situation, there is a 'give and take' clause that comes about automatically, sometimes without our full knowledge; it has a great deal to do with the 'karma' of our lifetimes.

My belief in giving anything at all to anyone, from friendship to money, is that it should be given freely, without restrictions, or not given at all because by imposing petty restrictions, it *stints* the personal thinking of the person receiving it and the giver receives power, instead of an opening of the heart, alongside good, positive *karma.*

Dee and Bill, when they came to England, did not reside in the South West, at first, but stayed in various parts of the country, many miles from Somerset. Dee, having strong, developed instincts, moved according to the feel of where they should go and this, in time, brought them to Castle Cary, and then eventually to us at Ansford.

Knowing, when I met them, that there was a chance for them in this life of great spiritual advancement, or mortal pursuits, I tried to gently clear the way and many hours of discussion, with questions and answers, took place. Bill had the makings of a good healer; Dee complemented this with her 'instinct' abilities. I gave Bill the chance of finding Self–Realization, in this lifetime, for I was his Guru, unknown to him.

40

A Lesson Learnt

"MATA, I would like to hear you lecture to more people." I heard Daniel say.

"Why do you say that?" I asked, "We have so many spiritual activities running at the moment."

Daniel agreed, but said he would like to organise an evening for me to lecture, in one of the larger halls — would I allow him to do this? His fervour on the matter was great… I accepted, knowing the experience would be invaluable to him.

I am writing, in this book, many matters that I have not been allowed to divulge before, and here is one of them:

Before giving Daniel sanction to organise a talk at Bristol for me, I, as usual, went into meditation on it, to see if, as I felt, it was the right thing to do. I beheld Mahavatar Babaji, Yoganandaji and Sri Yukteswarji; Babaji spoke of his pleasure with the Centre and the love within it. Guruji then affirmed that a talk should be given in Bristol, that it would be full, to overflowing, but not everyone there would be seen. He said I must leave the S.R.F. Centre in America unspoken about and the part I was to play in this lifetime was also not to be talked about, for the present, until the time came when a book would be written. I queried this and asked, "Why did you choose me, I am not clever and cannot speak in Hindi".

Babaji replied, "You are not wanted for your churches and certainly we do not wish you to speak in Hindi", they went on, each adding their thoughts, "We have chosen you for your love, speak of *THIS* love from the heart". Guruji then added, as he had been given a mission abroad, in America, so I had mine, in England — to forget what I had been and concentrate on whom I now *AM*.

There was such joy in my heart, on hearing their words.

Guruji then said he was bestowing a further name on me, that of Dharma… truth. They spoke of my knowledge, of my love for them and God — light, that my Wisdom would be infallible, though often in humbleness, I would question the verity of it.

I was asked by Sri Yukteswarji, not to baffle people with all my names, but only to tell them to true devotees; using one or two in everyday life. They reinforced what had already been said to me before, to teach not only from their wisdom, but also my own, taking evolution a step further. I wished that we could talk and stay forever as we were then, but too soon they were gone and I was there pondering on each word that had been spoken.

Daniel hired St. George's Hall in Bristol, for one evening; he had the tickets, the helpers and publicity to organise, he spared himself nothing. Nini Davies volunteered to sing a beautiful carol with a friend of hers, before my talk; after the talk we were going to finish with a chant *I AM LOVE… I AM PEACE*. Rowena and Keith supplied the musical backing for this, which was played on a keyboard.

"Shall I record this for you?" asked Ian Pringle.

Daniel accepted this kind offer, and with Christy Bradfords flair for setting the stage scene with flowers… we were ready.

"Do you think we shall have many people coming?" Daniel asked me.

"Yes, we will have all the people we need." I replied.

There is no luck in life, everything that matters has already been put into the universal energy, ready to be used, or produced at the correct time.

The day arrived; the atmosphere was charged with *anticipation*. The sky had opened to produce torrential rain, that continued for many hours, but this did not daunt us.

As the carol was finishing, I walked and took my place on the stage, a large, friendly chair awaited me. *Noticing only* the peace in the hall I began my talk with the most important word in the Universe, *LOVE.*

The beauty of the evening was evident and I was told the talk was enjoyed. We had approximately fifty people whom we could see, but many more present… with us… that most could not see. A great sadness enveloped me as we sang *I am love… I am Peace.*

This had come to me, to be used as the Centre's chant. The words have a great depth to them and yet as I sang these words on that particular evening, I knew and felt the void of love and peace in the whole Universe.

Many lessons were to be learnt from that night, for those involved. First — that it is quality and not quantity that matters. Second — (because I started my talk before the last carol had been sung) we learn, that we go ahead with whatever flows through us at the time and that it should be God's will be done, not our will be done. Third — to enjoy every moment of everything, without *criticism.*

Daniel also learnt about advertising and promotion, which would hold him in good stead for the future and therefore enable him to add more attributes of his own to the Centre.

I learnt, once more, if one is immersed in God and Guru, then anything can be done, including singing in public; *Deo Gratis.*

Let us treat
All of Creation
With respect

41

Disciples and Gurus

NOT all disciples recognise their Gurus, but without fail, the Guru recognises them, and works from the distance that is imposed upon them, putting in light whenever possible. The day that the relationship is recognised by both parties, that is the time that the disciple pushes forward in his or her spiritual progress.

A person can have many teachers over the years, but there is only one Guru for them in a lifetime.

One cannot push anyone into the path of Self–Realization, only help them to help themselves.

A Guru has the power to intervene, but only when asked.

To devotional disciples, who love and acknowledge the 'light' within their master, they will, with the wisdom given to them, find themselves and become as one, with God — the light of life.

There is a saying that 'we can only recognise the *level* of ourselves in others'. We cannot be *WISER* than we are at that given moment of time, and therefore if someone who is wiser tells us something we do not understand, we think they are wrong. As this is a fact of life, we need to pray, to find someone who is wiser and *egoless,* whom we can put our trust and faith in, 'temporarily', while we find our *Higher SELVES* [20]. Once you can *tune into this Higher Self* which is one of the highest communications, we then have ready access to Wisdom. This access would be dangerous to yourself and others whilst still maintaining vast egos. In youth, we need our ego, it carries us forward in life, to accomplishments of varied degrees. With a 'big head' we feel the world is at our feet, nothing seems impossible. Later on in life, when we have reached a mature age, we do not need our ego any longer, we need peace, love and wisdom; it is so noticeable how ego–minded people lack this love and understanding.

The big problem is, to see when it is time to let this ego go; we become attached to it, like an old friend, we know it well. To let this ego go, would leave us without any defences; yes it would, but you have to let go of one friend to get another, perhaps wiser friend… like Wisdom. Once we have seen and made a firm decision, that we wish to be rid of this ego, we can try to do it ourselves — how can we though? Do we always, if ever, see and acknowledge our own ego?… others yes, but it is far more difficult to see our own.

Hence, we need a 'Dispeller of Darkness' a Guru. *Gu* — meaning dispeller, *Ru* — the darkness.

In this day and age, the word guru has lost much of its status. There are gurus of cheese, gurus of the garden, gurus of 'red tape'; perhaps the name and word will not remain for long in existence, even though the word, taken correctly, is very beautiful as are so many of a 'like' nature. People ask how can I find such a person, and how can they be identified?

Bearing in mind, that as other professions have their charlatans, so does the spiritual life; they are called self–made gurus, well meaning people, perhaps, but nevertheless dangerous ones. They are people who have acquired knowledge usually from books and teachers, feel they would like to teach, are attracted to the word guru, and use it for themselves.

Most true Gurus do not seek to be one and very rarely feel that they are adequate, in their own eyes, to fit that sacred given name; I say given, for it can only be bestowed upon one.

To speak harshly on the subject of those who take the name guru and are not given it, must be, for the dangers of such an unauthorised person are great, to themselves, and others.

How *DO* we find such a person — a true Guru?

One asks with sincerity, and with deep devotion, to meet such a person, and then waits… and waits, until in God's time, they will come. If then, you go in faith and trust with that person, all will be well. If you try to impose your will on theirs, you can only hurt yourself.

To recognise one is more difficult, for they come in all disguises, both male and female. Do not look for flowing robes and long hair; if you think it is these things that make such a person, you are wrong, look at their eyes and hands. If the eyes are still and loving, the hands at peace, resting, only to make gentle movements when required — look further and your heart should then convey to you the answer. Once found, stay with them, do not try to make a better mixture, with teachers and Gurus; listening to *SPIRITUAL ADVICE* from different voices, does not make a good mix — for you, and you will be torn in many directions… finding no direction.

Now, more young people than ever before are searching for the truth; they will find it, but the mountain is high — there are rocks and boulders, as well as green pastures. No one would go mountaineering, up an unknown mountain, without a guide… would they?

We have within us
The Finest Computer

42

More Revelations

WHEN people say that they have seen Ji Jesus's face, talked to a saint, or been comforted by a saintly soul, it could be true — why not? They come in times of need, when people need a helping hand; no more than you would, for a friend in trouble.

There is no separation between them and us, only a brighter light or our inability to raise ourselves to a high energy level. Ji Jesus has, from time to time, soothed my brow and spoken words of comfort to me, but only when in *need*.

I have seen and even spoken to the baby boy I lost, he is well and happy.

Captain, our dog, whom we had to 'put to sleep' because of his suffering, I have spoken to and stroked his beautiful coat that was once scarred and unhealthy. These happenings can be natural and can happen by seeing with our two eyes, while awake, or in our dreamless state — but are we not alive while we are dreaming, and dreaming, while alive!

One sunny day, I took a walk, feeling the need to stretch my legs and commune with nature. I felt a desire to turn down a particular lane called Talbot Lane, this led into other lanes with fields on either side. Finding a large slab of stone to sit on, I rested and listened to the silence around.

My thoughts turned to the Centre and the feeling of change taking place. There was a surge of unrest, as my thoughts continued; a feeling that we were going to move again, expansion... excitement… all these thoughts and yet, no reason for them, letting them waft away with the slight breeze around me. I started to walk back, taking a longer route, to make the most of the sunshine. My way took me past a lovely old house, standing in its own grounds. I stood, to look at it once again, admiring its shrubs and trees and I heard an inner, silent voice proclaiming that soon we would move to a house this size within our own grounds, and I would know it by its door knocker and by a vision I had of it, a while ago. Suddenly, it came back to me, a picture of a large, long house, an old one, with Georgian casement windows and a driveway; this house had a driveway, but it was not the one. But, how could we move, we had no money — and why? We could only just manage with all the work we had, where we lived now; many questions and no answers.

I knew the best thing to do now, would be to remain still, within and without, till the answer came, but I had to try something, so I put a note in their door, to see if they were thinking of selling. Of course they were not and I *had* to wait patiently for my answer.

This came one morning, after my meditation. I was sitting quietly imbibing the peace, when my Guru suddenly made his presence felt.

"What is your hurry?" he asked.

"What hurry?" I replied.

"The house will come without you pushing for it," He continued, "It is your destiny and therefore it will take place."

On hearing this, I started to ask him more questions.

"Hush, not so many questions, please — listen to me and you will learn more that way!"

I was about to question him more, but he interrupted me quickly asking me to wait till the right time, when, I would know what to do.

"Do you have faith?" he asked.

With this, I fell to my knees and asked forgiveness for my questioning him.

With his inimitable chuckle, he was gone, and I sat bewildered, but excited at the same time… and waited.

43

German T. V.

*Y*ET another television network wanted to film the Centre and its activities; this time, they wanted much larger animals and if possible, a vet. with whom they could conduct an interview.

We had been visiting, and giving healings, not only to people, but also to a good range of animals who lived near Guildford, Surrey. The family we visited had a large farmhouse, set in its own grounds; a perfect place for the TV crew to come and film. On asking the family if they would permit it, and receiving the answer "Yes, do come," we set off early one morning for the start of the day's 'shoot'.

Our last time in Guildford had been several weeks before, when we had given healing to a horse that had a painful condition in his fetlock and could not be ridden. The Vet had promised he would not administer drugs until we came down again; because of this situation, our visit was of particular interest to us.

When we set out, it was raining and a cold wind whistled around the car — we arrived to an open log fire and refreshments for all, worthy of a king.

The horse had much improved and was now able to trot. The Vet had kept his promise and was himself interviewed. He told us he was impressed at how the healing had improved the horse's condition without any further medical treatment.

All in all, it was a progressive day; the TV crew got their film of a horse having a healing as well as a good interview and we were thrilled, once more, to see yet another of God's creatures become whole. Animals are so open to love and the healing energy; they put no barriers up so therefore it leaves them open to receive fully of *THE POWER.*

I wish that Humans were the same.

Look within
for
Peace
Love
Wisdom

44

My Name Dharma

and

Alpha–Omega Family Now

THE Meditation groups and classes were expanding rapidly now; the difficulty in keeping them on a one to one basis, with so many people wanting to learn meditation, made me realise they would now have to be in small groups, but never so big that I would be unable to minister to the individual.

I loved and treasured these times, more than written words could ever express. Now, I knew where my heart lay, what my search had been all about… Meditation and its teachings. Healings and any aspect of it, cooking, cleaning, or discussion, I loved them all, but Meditation was my true ultimate life's work.

After the group Meditations had finished, I always sat as long as possible, imbibing the peace; on one of these occasions, Guruji came to me. He had seen my difficulty in hiding the truth, yet not telling a lie, when my class enquired about my Guru.

"You are doing what I ask of you," he said, "and doing well with the Meditation classes. You are a great lover of the truth — because of this the last name I gave you was 'Dharma' which stands for Truth. When you move from here, as you will, once more, I ask your family to be called the Alpha–Omega family; this will go into your mind to be forgotten until the day it is needed, to be remembered."

Guruji had already said that this family would be the first of its kind and would not last if it was not built on unconditional love, so Alpha–Omega... meaning the first and last, seemed a very appropriate name to have.

"Thank you Guruji." I said, but before I had finished, he had gone once more.

45

Our New Receptionist

MY love for Daniel — my spiritual son, is great and he is doing so well now — how blessed I am. I desire to share the knowledge I have for him, but it must wait — for the time is not right yet.

"Mata, we could do with someone on the reception desk." This was Daniel reminding me that as we were all healing now, we had no one to answer the telephone, or look after our patients in our small waiting room.

"Will you put a notice up in the waiting room, please." I said, "Then perhaps someone may see it who would like to help us." At that time we could not afford to pay a receptionist.

This was duly done, and we waited.

Christine Bradford had been in and out of the Centre for a while now; at first she had suffered severely with osteoarthritis. As she overcame this illness, she became interested in Meditation and asked me if I would teach her. This I did, knowing that she would become important in our lives; I would spend more time with her, taking her in advance of her knowledge at all times, when she would allow it. Fighting a great battle within herself, she also fought me and would sometimes disappear for weeks, and then come again to see me. We were playing a divine game of Guru and disciple, but as the disciple does not recognise the Guru, more often than not, this is the way of it and it can continue from one second, through weeks, months, years or lifetimes, before the devotee will see the light and the truth; meanwhile the Guru will 'fish' and wait patiently for as long as it takes.

Christine was unhappy, for she was used to doing everything for herself and felt *this* Meditation, she could do on her own as well — so she suffered, while I waited with outstretched arms.

Christine's children, Keith and Tracey[21] both came for healings, and they both impressed me with their inner spirituality.

The notice for a receptionist had been up for a week or more, when Christine, very hesitantly, asked if she would be suitable for the job. Bearing in mind her obstinacy and strong will, which is good material for a healer, when 'fired' and 'tempered' properly, I said, "Yes, we would love to have you, but we have no money, as yet, to pay anyone."

"I do not want paying," was her reply, "Just the job."

"When could you start?" I asked.

"Tomorrow." was the reply. It did not take us long to see how good Christine was at reception and a joy to have with us.

Daniel found her a joy as well, and after a few months, he came to inform me that they both loved each other — he knew their loving friendship would have to remain so for a while till she could marry him, but he was prepared to wait for her as long as need be.

Yet another part of the Infinite's plan completed.

I willingly gave my blessing to this partnership, for I had known for a long time that they were meant for each other, though the timing of their getting together, was in the Infinite's hands. Christine told me she liked to be called Christy, and as she had progressed greatly, I felt the name befitted her now, and so she became Christy and one of the family.

46

Ian and Nini

*T*HE Centre was now getting well known, not only in England, Wales and Scotland, but also abroad in Europe, Africa, India and other Asian countries. Meanwhile, we would have calls from visitors to this country from America, wishing to see the Centre and quite often staying a few days to have healings.

Young people started taking more interest in our talks and lectures and the age limit of interest was getting lower as the months flew by.

It was about this time that Ian Pringle and Nini Davies came into our lives. One day there was a knock on our door; Nini and Ian introduced themselves as acupuncturists who lived and had their practice in Wells.

"Would you like to see the Centre?" I asked them.

"Yes, we would." They replied.

"We are not healing at present, so I will be able to show you the healing rooms as well." I added.

At our first encounter, I recognised them, but they did not recognise me. I believe as we spoke of energies and the power of our minds, that they were slightly bewildered, for I was threatening their long held beliefs, so I was very gentle with them; we said our *au revoirs* and they went on their way.

Shortly after our meeting, they rang up and booked in for a healing appointment; I booked them in with myself, for it was necessary to get to know them better and they… me. It seemed that they had been working acupuncturists for several years now, and though having only a small practice, were very busy with a steady flow of patients. They lived and worked together, and made a good team.

They were vegetarians bordering on vegans and had an organic garden full of vegetables; they had been through the 'mill of life' and were now ready for further progress.

Our conversations were always alive and their minds sorted and sifted as we spoke on many different subjects. Knowing of their appetite for spiritual food, I asked them, "Would you like to learn Meditation, one that would feed every part of you?"

"Yes, we would like to do it, if it is possible?" they replied.

"Come each week," I said, "and I will teach and guide you." As the weeks passed, they learnt and absorbed the Meditation. Being apt and willing pupils, they then wished to have more knowledge on other spiritual subjects, so our discourses continued over the months.

It took time for them to see me properly, as their humble Guru who had loved them in a past life, and was here to pick up the threads once more, for it was also known to me that they had rejected the teachings in their last living existence... and I had to wait a little longer for them... to meet again in this lifetime.

In the *Autobiography of a Yogi*, written by my Guru, it explains how all this takes place. I used to ask Guruji and now once more repeated my question, "Why make me a woman in this lifetime?" He answered me one day, saying, "We do not want you for the multitudes, but for the few who desire and are ready for further spiritual progress. If you are hidden in a woman's body and are not outstandingly pretty and live in the country, you will be harder to find and they will have to pray and look harder for you, for their much needed guidance." He went on, "I have told you that you were a man in your previous existence"; but this time he went further and commenced to tell me who I had been. When he had finished, I asked him, "Why are you telling me this now?"

"You will need to know;" he replied, "For you will have much work to do with souls and this knowledge will help you — retain this knowledge, but do not use it." were his loving words which I have kept to and will do so as long as it is wished of me.

The information on our past lives is not given lightly and should not be sought. It will come naturally to any person who is in need of this knowledge; it also brings a responsibility with it — to get on with one's life as we are, man or woman in this lifetime, and not make the knowledge we have attained of ourselves into the most prime important factor. Likewise, to receive without asking, from a Higher Source (our Higher Self, or Master), we can be certain it will be the truth; from a lesser source, there is always a possibility of make–believe.

Perhaps now, I need not ask this question again.

Ian and Nini were close to me now and as we prepared our talks and discussion groups, they would be quite happy to come and help. Ian had a good head for engineering and building projects with the ability of a draughtsman as well. I was not surprised, there-fore, when he later informed me he liked computers and had an old sewing machine which he used for making coats, trousers and dresses — a self–contained DIY person.

Nini had a birdlike voice of many tones and sang regularly at Wells Cathedral — she also had a quick wit and a way of writing that was to hold her in good stead for the future; a keen gardening ability was also in evidence.

Having dinner with them, one evening at their home, on their return from Greece, we spoke of the Centre's progress and of the desire to build, if and when it needed a bigger building. Ian was immediately interested and gave an offer of his services, if we needed him. We were yet to realise how valuable this offer would be to us in the very near future.

"Guruji, would you give us a blessing and officiate at our wed-ding, and may we have it at the Centre?" Ian and Nini came in to ask me this question one day. I was delighted to be asked and agreed that I would participate in whatever way they wished. They invited a few of their friends and asked that it could be held in the Meditation room, which was a fairly large, peaceful room with pale mauve walls and an old Indian carpet with beanbags around the room for sitting on. Here Nini and Ian made their vows to each other, a ceremony befitting a spiritual partnership took place, followed by a quiet tea–sipping downstairs.

The marriage was made in heaven (within), but how many are? A slip of paper does not make a true marriage — there is the needed financial support that the paper gives, but true soul marriages are usually made between the most unlikely people, but usually ones who know — come what may — that their destinies are linked together for this lifetime.

These are the youngsters who will make and show the importance of trust in the divine will and in themselves. I am not saying that in my lifetime *all* will see it this way, but more marriages are made on earth by mental and emotional feelings than in heaven by spiritual ones.

IT WILL COME IN TIME.

47

Plans for the Future

ONE cannot do extremely hard physical work every day and remain in a deep blissful state at all times —this would be dangerous as the levels are so different. During such physical times, I would refrain from *this* state, but still be at the level of peace state which can be maintained at all times, easily. When the Self-Realization state has been reached, one misses the depth of communion, but it is wise to refrain. When such physical work is completed, the level can be deepened again.

It was after Meditation one evening, I had looked at myself and the day, and was now contemplating the wonders of life when I felt my Guruji with me; he wished to speak with me on an important matter.

My answer was given in great love. "With Infinite delight." I replied. There was silence for a little while, then he told me a story.

"Once upon a time, there was a traveller who had a long distance to go to her destination. She had been to this said destination a long time ago, but the memory of it was dimmed. She asked a guard at the station if he would tell her the train times and give her all the information needed to take this journey. This having been done, she waited for the train. It was a train of many compartments, each compartment being different within itself. To make the time pass quickly while travelling on this train, she studied life in all its different compartments, reviving memories, meeting old friends.

Sooner than expected, her destination, for that journey, was reached.

"The sun shone, the pastures were green and inviting, with animals abounding everywhere in their own habitats. With people of love and laughter and no discord around her, she made plans to make her permanent home here, in this rarefied place of wonderment.

"As the time passed, though finding work to do there, this happiness was not making her content; there are many people, she thought, who know nothing of this way of life. They do not even know that there is a train; that, taking this train journey, with knowledge about it, would bring them to peace and happiness; her heart was heavy, a big cloud of sadness enveloped her whole being.

"I must return, she thought, it is not sufficient to be at peace, and happy, while others suffer. Next day she booked a seat on the train back to where she was needed, keeping the peace, love and joy always *WITHIN* her."

As Guruji finished, I knew what he was saying — that if I stayed quietly in my own world, people would see only an 'aloofness' in me — not seeing clearly, they would fear the unknown person they were seeing. I must hide myself well, for the time being, inwardly, and yet be more mortal outwardly, to each as they need me.

Guruji went on to say, each stage of evolution needs a different ingredient and that now *all* the past experiences were going to be put to good use.

"Surely," I asked him, "This could be done by someone else more qualified?" — I never felt adequate for what was asked of me.

"Love is the only needed qualification," he replied, "That you have other attributes, is just an added bonus."

"What is this task to be?" I ventured.

"I want you to prepare a thought to become a Cooperative" he continued, "I use this word to give you perspective. In reality, it will be a loving family of six to eight people, all from different backgrounds, praying, living and working together, as one, showing the world that this can be done... and will *eventually* be so — it shall be called the Alpha-Omega family. They must be shown and guided by you, for you were chosen for this task a long time ago." Paramahansaji went on to say, "The new Centre will come about in the near future, you will recognise it by the windows and door knocker." Saying this, he gave me a mental picture of it telling me to hold it in my mind's eye.

"But Guruji, there must be others to do this work," I said. "I do not like being in charge of anything, or anyone."

"Exactly," he replied, "Even better."

I had hoped, and prayed, that after much of my lifetime being spent in running and organising people and events, that I would be allowed to melt into a sublime oblivion, obviously this was not going to happen.

"You will be Guru to many souls" Guruji continued, "And you will be asked to do *MUCH* to hasten these souls along. Go in faith, for your love and wisdom will never fail you."

Having heard this, I now felt more at peace with what my Guru was asking of me.

"Will the Centre grow into a large one, like yours did?" I ventured to ask.

"No," was the reply, "This will be a smaller Centre with rays of light extending out to all corners of the earth; it must not get too large, or the *love* quality may suffer," He went on to say, "This Centre must be full of *love*, it is the first Centre of its kind."

"Guruji," I said humbly, "Do you mean that unless we are all full of unconditional love — it will not last?"

"Yes." he replied.

I lovingly queried his remark of "being the very first family of unconditional love", for I wanted to understand his words correctly.

"There are many, but not of *unconditional* love," was his answer. "It is time, and you must work with them as I have with you. Take those that you recognise and fire them into good tools."

After speaking to me then, on more personal matters about the future, he blessed me and with a gentle smile, he departed.

Having already accepted all he had said into my heart, I now ceased feeling apprehensive, while a great joy filled my being.

48

The Right Time

"CAN we have a word with yourself and Peter?" Bill asked one day towards the end of a day's healing.

"Yes, we can come now, if it is convenient." Peter said in reply, and wondering what the summons was all about, we hastily made our way over from the Centre, to the house.

Bill started by saying, "We want to live abroad, we have found a house in Spain, so we need to sell the Centre and this house, would you like to buy them, or perhaps, just the Centre?"

We asked if we could think this over as there were many thoughts going through our heads, not least of all was Guruji's prophesy of a move.

We were very grateful to Dee and Bill for all their help, but we also saw the upsurge of minor crime and drunkenness that was becoming more apparent in Castle Cary — we declined Bill's offer and with faith, waited. With no money and no apparent means of getting any... I just wondered what the Infinite, or my Guru were 'up to'.

Telling the patients we would have to leave the premises soon was not a pleasant task for us to have to do, we told them each individually so that they understood we did not want to desert them, only we had no choice. They understood and stood by us till the time came to leave.

Mrs Joyce Pratt and her husband, Harold, who lived at Old Farm, South Barrow, had become very good friends of ours and we would spend our leisure time in the evenings with them, talking over life in general.

Harold had now passed on into another life; Joyce was continuing in life, always helping someone.

One day Joyce said to us, very straight to the point as she always was, "Go and find a house that you like and I will buy it for you, as a present".

"But we can't do that." I replied, "We haven't got any money at all to put towards it, we can't let you do this."

"Nonsense," she replied, "Harold would like me to do this for you both, and your work must continue."

Knowing Joyce meant what she said, we decided to look. Several houses were looked at and we saw one large house but fortunately for us it was not available, nor did it have the correct windows or door knocker!

One day we went for a walk around Castle Cary — there was a postal strike on at the time, and as we passed an Estate Agent, my eyes saw a large coloured photograph of a lovely big old house and my heart missed a beat... no, it can't be, was my first thought. I quickly told Peter about the photograph of the house as we passed on and he said, let's go back then, and look at it again. We did, we looked, we got a brochure and I knew this was the house — but the price? We asked the Agent if anyone had seen it yet, "Oh, no," was the reply, "It's only just come on the market and of course the postal strike does not help."

The following day we showed the brochure to Joyce who said, "Let's go and see it," and we did.

We had been through Queen Camel many times and had never seen this house; one of the largest in the village, it lies off the main road at the end of a lane. It has a short driveway and the 17th Century farmhouse extends the full length of the driveway with Georgian casement windows and a large garden with a paddock of two acres. At the back were flowers, shrubs and trees to feast our eyes on, and on the front door – 'the knocker of my vision'.

"It's our house," I said, "It's the house and door knocker I saw in a vision some time ago."

"Are you sure?" Peter said.

"You must be sure," said Joyce, "Before we get involved."

"I am absolutely sure." I replied.

The rooms were spacious inside with a large lounge, dining room, study and a large kitchen downstairs and five bedrooms upstairs with bathrooms; I noted a well in the garden, which added to its uniqueness. We were the first to view and so proceeded to purchase.

There were problems to try us and setbacks to only make us more firm in our decision; then… eventually, the house was ours.

Our happiness, in the knowledge that this was the *RIGHT* house and spiritually meant for us now, was a humbling experience and once more was to test my faith before everything was signed and sealed.

Daniel and Christy had already said that they would like to be part of our family — "Please could our children come too?" asked Christy.

"Of course," I replied, "Your children are our children."

"And one dog," said Christy, "He's a Collie whom I rescued from being badly treated — he's Sammy."

Sammy, a Collie, Charka and Gemmy, two Jack Russells, "that sounds a good mix to start with," I said; what Christy did not know was that I had always wanted a Collie dog.

It seemed all my prayers were being answered at once. What could I say, except renew my love and faith in God and Guru, as I had done before.

There is
no finer love
than
Unconditional Love

49

A Charity

*J*OYCE could not buy the house for us in Queen Camel, unless we became a charity; also, Joyce was only allowed to give us a certain sum of money before it became taxable — a tax Joyce knew we could not afford. Likewise, if she passed before a certain 'passage of years', we would have death duties to pay. This came as a shock to us, for though we had tried to become a charity before this, it seemed a never ending battle with 'red tape' all the way.

It was now in the hands of the solicitor; we assumed that there would be no more problems to beset us — we now had three months to go before our move. We told Joyce somehow *we would* be a charity by then; we asked her to trust us… she did.

The Solicitor, to our dismay, had our file just sitting on her desk. We took the matter out of her hands and started contacting the Charity Commission in London direct, only to find that they had mislaid all documents about us… we would have to start all over again, they said. With sinking hearts and numerous journeys to and from London… three days before our move, we became a charity.

Be
at
all times true
to
your Self

50

The Move

WITH the help of many friends, we hired a van and moved our furniture along with Christy's and Daniel's belongings, over a period of four days, in the middle of December 1988. We gave ourselves a week off from all duties, apart from unpacking and reallocating our furniture in our new Centre. The carpets were already there, so our task was that much easier than our last move; the curtains would come later. Our healing rooms were to be the lounge and the two bedrooms upstairs, which were suitable for that purpose.

Our three dogs looked and sniffed, wanting to know more about each other, but I could see that Charka, though small in stature was determined… he was going to be boss and so he was and has remained so ever since. Sammy's first love we found to be food, so through his stomach, we found his heart. He had been starved when he was a younger dog and the memory of this episode in his life, however loved or well fed he is, remains with him in the form of a food addiction. Gemmy, a rounder smooth haired bitch, gentle, loving and slightly nervous, seemed to have no time for such goings on, as barking, fighting or eating — she loves company and that's it. So there we were, at last, the Denton Healing Centre, in its more beautiful surroundings with the first residents of the Alpha–Omega family, with more to come.

The house had been called *The Dring* and had, at one time, been a row of three farm cottages; it was later made into one building and bought by a Mrs Pope who is believed to be connected with Eldridge Pope & Sons, the Wine Merchants. Then the later owners, we were told, held dinner and tea parties with tennis afternoons — a grass court is nearby along with a rotating sun house, which is still in very good working condition, where they would take their breaks from tennis playing.

Around the old tennis court there were hedges of beech and yew and to one side many trees of chestnut, ash, cherry, scots pine and hazel, which made the garden a secluded and peaceful one to be in. Passing the beech hedge, you come across a paddock that used to have horses and sheep grazing in it surrounded by further natural hedges and a cluster of young beech trees at the furthest point. Following on from this grassy half acre, there was a further expansion of land used for vegetables, with pear and apple trees in their wake.

Going through a small gate, the stables could be reached — there were three very old horse boxes which were well constructed, though well used in the past; then, on to a sun lounge of low, large proportions, with large old oak framed double doors. On to an old well which is full of water, but not in use at present, then into the back of the house where roses grow, taking up the bare wall space, along with wisteria. If you amble to the side of the house, there is a large pear tree and herb garden… but I must stop here and continue with our story.

We were soon working and in full swing, with the healing, courses, and other commitments, not forgetting the garden, which we had already fallen in love with. The housework and garden had to be done before 9 o'clock in the morning or after 8 o'clock in the evening. This was not feasible for very long and we started looking for someone to help with the housework. We asked Joyce, who had also moved and was now living in Queen Camel, only a short distance away from us, if she knew of anyone. "No, I have a good home help, but she is not for sale," said Joyce, with a twinkle in her eye.

We put a card in the shop window, up the road, and waited... working... hopefully. After a few days we had a phone call from a local woman called Shirley Shean.

"Can you come and see me?" I asked her.

"Yes, I can," she said and the next day a very happy looking, determined faced person turned into our gates on a bicycle, dismounting as I greeted her. We went into the house together to find out if we were suitable for each other; we soon found common ground and Shirley started work with us. She is a tower of strength, always seemingly happy and content and she looks after, not only the house, but us as well... and that is a 'tall order'.

"We really need more healing rooms and more space" — the family were having a discussion on the difficulties we were having, using the lounge and extra bedrooms as healing rooms. "We could use the sun lounge" suggested one member of the family, "Or build on to it" said another. Hearing this, my mind went to Ian and his draughtsman abilities. "I will ask Ian what he feels about this." I said, and we left the matter alone, while I made contact with him.

"Let's design and make a larger building." he replied, on hearing our thoughts.

"How long will it take then?" I asked, aware of the urgency of the matter.

"Not long, but it could cost a lot of money."

"That's impossible," I retorted "We haven't got any."

"I will draw up some plans," said Ian, "have a look at them and see what you think can be done."

Thanking him, I started to put this thought out — "we need this building", then I put a notice up for the patients to see, telling them of the need of an extension. Money started to come in from all sides and it was not long before we could consider the building of the healing block. Ian, knowing of our difficulties, said he would work when he could and had days to spare from his practice, but he would need a friend to help him he said, and asked Michael Eisele, who lived in Glastonbury. Michael could work full time, but Ian could only work two or three days a week.

We left the project to them — all we had to do was to raise sufficient money to enable Ian to keep buying the building materials and pay the wages. Both Ian and Michael took less wages, so as to help us and Christy and Daniel took only five pounds to ten pounds and sometimes not that, until we had finished the building.

We also had to call in a local builder for the erection of the stone walls and plastering, as this was a major job, and having this helped speed up the work. This made a great difference to Ian and Michael allowing them a freer hand to get on with the timber work.

Finishing the building in record time, the four of us started painting the rooms with colours that spoke to us, each room being a different colour. We almost had to do without carpets, until one day we had a large donation handed to us. We had wall lights made by the local potter and before long, the building was blessed and opened for patients from near and far and for any of the Infinite's beloved creatures in creation.

We had three healing–come–counselling rooms, a large waiting room with toilet and an animal healing room which had to double as an office for the moment.

51

Conversion

THE lounge was not only for sitting in, it was also where we had our morning and evening Meditations. From these meditations we were spiritually, mentally and physically fed and from these meditations and the love we found from them, we would then go and administer to others.

We can only allow the voltage through us of the healing power that we are capable of maintaining within, so our Meditations, with patience and perseverance, will make us into a more powerful transformer, which in its turn gives us more healing power... therefore making us better people and much more capable with our healing powers, in whatever context we use them.

One day, in one lifetime, we shall all put Meditation *into* our life and then the world will become loving and peaceful, once more.

Sometimes, we would have people staying with us, who wanted to have the lounge to themselves, reading by the open fire, or playing records of a tranquil nature. At these times, we would have to find alternate places to meditate — why not — except it profits those who are learning and on the path of meditation, to meditate together with us, opening our own hearts and doors to all others who wish to join us at these very special times.

We had a long, wide garage adjoining the house — would this do for a Meditation room we wondered.

"Michael could help me make it into one." Ian said.

"It must be a very special one." The family retorted.

Ian, thoughtful before replying, said "Yes, it will be, I have always wanted to create and build something different in the way of a Meditation room."

He became very enthusiastic and said he would draw up plans for the room, including the stained glass windows, that he would make especially for it. The idea sounded a perfect solution to our problem — the plans looked unusually good, so with skimping and saving, Ian and Michael once more started on another building project.

The Meditation room took well over a year to finish, with the painting and seat covers being finished with Christy and Nini's helping hands.

The Meditation room was finished at last, and looked very beautiful, representing at the same time, the Eastern and Western cultures, incorporating all religions, yet no religion… just a 'way of life'.

52

The Family Grows

*O*NE day, quite suddenly, I knew I had to ask Ian and Nini if they would like to be part of our family.

Permission from a higher level had to be asked, for it was a little ahead of 'the spiritual schedule'. The answer came "yes, it could be done, but it would be more difficult for you for a few months".

"Would it harm others?" I asked inwardly.

"No, just more work for yourself."

Weighing this up, I knew for the sake of Christy, Daniel and Peter that I must ask them and take all responsibility for it.

When we next met, I asked Ian and Nini if they would like to join us and become part of our family, knowing it was not spiritually, officially the right time. I was not surprised to find lack of enthusiasm. They knew I was their Guru and we loved each other... but this was different.

What a struggle took place within themselves.

To find Self–Realization in this lifetime, they had wanted and asked for, but now... it meant selling their house, being beholden to others, as well as themselves, not being able to take days off and holidays at will and... no security... except 'all the security anyone needs — God's security'.

They would have a ready–made family, my unconditional, undying everlasting love, but they were young and wanted all the mortal things as well. They knew well the proverb 'Give all, to receive all' and believed this, but they fought the longing to come 'tooth and nail'.

"I would like to be with you Mataji", Ian said, "But would like to see India first."

Nini wanted to give me her answer on their return, but knowing she was like a well–bred mule, that had to be tethered for a little while for her own good, I asked to have her reply before they departed, adding that we would help them financially if it were at all possible. Meanwhile their house would go up for sale and on their return they would come and be part of the Alpha–Omega family. They had tried living in a community before this, had found it lacking and departed from it, so they had trepidations this time, and had to put their faith completely in myself as their Guru and everything that I had told them. I did not underestimate what they had to do to come to us, but I knew of their future paths to come and the wonderful life that lay ahead of them, when the ground work has been done, for this was written in the stars and skies, so must take place — unless it is possible to change the skies and stars?!

"Before you go on holiday, Ian, I wish to give you the name Micheal, instead of Ian — will you accept this as your spiritual name, to attain to, as you are no longer an Ian and it will not help your progress by keeping to it?"

I said this, hoping he would take it, as a spiritually given name is not always given at the time of attainment, but sometimes before spiritual attainment, to help attain advancement more quickly — if it is needed. It can only be given by their Guru, or Master, and only knowingly when it is ordained so.

"Yes, I would like to have the name, as I don't feel like an Ian any longer, but neither do I feel like a Micheal."

His reply made, I wondered what his family would think, or anyone for that matter who did not understand the ways of the spiritual life.

Soon, they were off on their travels, eleven weeks travelling to India via America and Canada, with their haversacks on their backs — wearing their boots and in their shorts, we saw them off.

Christy and Daniel, having always had complete faith that this Centre was meant to come into being, got on with the hard work ahead of them and worked happily on any project given to them.

We could never have managed without the many people that came to help us make a start in our new Centre. Whether it was to cook, wash, iron or garden, we were always in need and still are, of these wonderful helpers. The Receptionist's work is always difficult and this was a post not everyone felt it possible to perform adequately. After all… whoever sits at the reception desk has a great responsibility with answering the telephone, making appointments for patients and generally overseeing the days events around the 'waiting room'. And what about the most needed smile and caring way that these people need to have. Need I say more!

We must
Think, Hope
and have Faith
To move mountains

53

A Marriage

"WE would like to make our vows to each other"… this was Daniel and Christy asking me to marry them and to give them a spiritual blessing while they made their commitment to each other.

Words cannot express the supreme joy I felt, and love for them both as my spiritual son and daughter. To be asked to do this made me feel very humble indeed, for I was being allowed to do the Infinite's beloved work, I could ask for no more than that.

"Can it be soon please?" They asked.

Knowing they believed there is a right sanctified time for everything, I asked them to wait till the time came of its 'own accord' — it did, with this knowledge making itself known only just a few hours beforehand.

Each marriage is so individual that only at the moment of time does the power feed and guide me in what to say and do.

With Tracey, Keith and Peter present, Christy and Daniel were married as surely as *I am* today — and in God's presence, they made their vows to love all as themselves, to work for the good of all, and to cherish all as in the one Light.

God that is life, that is Omnipresent, and that is unconditional love, will prevail throughout the Universe… *IN TIME… OM*

*Life is good
Perhaps sometimes the people
are not!*

54

We Make It Six

ON Nini and Micheal's return from India, our family took a
different turn — for the better. We had more help, but
also more love to give and receive.

It takes perhaps five years for a marriage to find its feet properly, and I believe with new found families, like ours, it must also
take a little time — if it can be quicker all well and good, if not,
knowing that it's my role to play, I accept whatever happens quite
happily, knowing the outcome to be perfectly planned for us, it just
needs our happy participation to make it *SO*.

We could now start running the Centre with wise decisions
being made by the whole family — an early rise for Meditation,
exercises and walking, then a meeting at 8.30 am to plan a skeleton
day, leaving plenty of room for changes as they are bound to
happen.

We all had our set duties besides our spiritual work, which we
alternated each day, when possible, so that each member of the
family learnt to do everything from cooking through the range, to
gardening. We all had a say on all matters and went forward on a
majority decision; perhaps I should have been called an arbiter at
these meetings!

The talents in the family were many, and we discovered that
we could be as a family, fairly self sufficient, with all its attributes
and yet, humble enough to see any faults. As in any family, the parents let the younger ones learn and find out for themselves, some-

times bearing the burden of their progressive lessons; this family was no different and the situations that they set up unknowingly for themselves, were many and wondrous, with hard lessons to learn. Peter was looking after the financial side and I was keeping the rest under my wing, until such time came that I could share the responsibility.

The Centre was growing… our courses for Healing, Meditation, Yoga, Spiritual Knowledge and Philosophy were full. More people were coming with stress related illnesses, cancer, heart, MS, arthritis and many others — all would come and stay for periods of rest and healings.

Meditation as opposed to meditative state had to be held back, for it was not time for its full release yet, though meditative states do have a great beneficial effect on those who use them.

The courses on Meditation that we did have… I took, knowing that soon I must relinquish all.

We still only had one room that we let people stay in and this concerned us greatly as the need was there and not being met adequately. Our office was a small room in which we all had to write, type and do other work during the day — it was not possible to work like this, so we had to use our bedrooms for our own means of writing, typing and copying. I had to find a suitable answer to these problems, but how to solve them — I did not know — I prayed and meditated and after my Meditations I would think on these matters, once more seeing the need for more money for any more projects that would come along.

I waited with a positive, calm mind, knowing that soon all would be made clear to me — but it seemed like eternity, although in reality it was only a few months.

55

Problem Solved

W HILE having a meeting with our Solicitor one day, we found to our chagrin that we could do no more to our property without the permission of the previous owner and his daughter in South Africa. Our dealings with him over the house had not been easy, and I knew any further requests for planning permission would meet with more of the same reaction.

Though we had a good two acres of land now, the whole acreage used to be a lot more, but it was sold off, the greater part of the estate now consisting of two cottages, a bungalow and a new house built adjacent to our boundary. We knew we would not be allowed further building permission while held to this extremely silly clause, but could we buy this new house — just completed, over the high wall from us? This was the only way I could see of getting rid of a clause that enabled someone to dictate to us, even though the Centre was ours with freehold.

You see, I had to find the money and buy this house for the future of the Centre, and by buying the house, the clause would automatically be removed, safeguarding the family and the Centre.

I felt compelled to mention this to Joyce, who agreed the clause was scandalous and had to go.

"I can help you," Joyce said, "But can you get a mortgage for the rest of the money that you will need?"

"Yes, I can and I will." I replied, thinking, here we go again. All my life I have had to spend, before the money is in my hands; perhaps tests of faith, to try me!

I also knew that the rest of our family must not have any of the burdens of money worries, for their work was to work on themselves for the future of other souls. Knowing this, Peter and myself went to find out about getting a mortgage.

We got the best bargain we could, but still with high interest to pay. We negotiated for the house and got it, thereby freeing the family of its 'clause' burden. We had enough furniture from Micheal and Nini's home, plus some of our own given to us by patients, to furnish the house, now called the Lodge.

No sooner had we furnished it then more people wanted to come and stay with us. Two members of the family lived over there and we had room now to have friends and relatives to stay, or anyone needing help. All this was wonderful, but the mortgage was a problem — not to worry about, but to think about. At the end of the year we received a large donation for the Centre, which just enabled us to pay off the whole mortgage and be free of all debts, once again.

Not long after moving to Laurel Lane, I quietly suggested that the family should have a name. We talked over different names until the Alpha–Omega popped out of my memory computer as rapidly as I had forgotten it... *Thus it was so.*

56

Home and Away

NOW, Peter was the regional Chairman for the National Federation of Spiritual Healers and myself the Vice Chairman and Training Officer of the Region — for my sins, and hereby lies the story.

The then Chairman and Vice Chairman of the region of Somerset, Avon and Gloucestershire, could not continue any longer and came to see us, asking if we could take up these respective positions. We both said no, as the extra work, which it would entail, could take us away from the responsibilities of our Centre.

Though concerned about the region being without a Chairman, they said they understood and no more was said on the subject. The AGM came looming up and we got ourselves ready to go, saying to each other *quite* firmly, that we would not be pressured into any post, now vacant.

We sat listening without saying a word, until the re-election of a Chairman came up and that is when I had the most odd feeling come over me, one of calm, but extreme heat generated itself throughout the whole of my body. I heard the words, "Would anyone take the position of Chairman?" — after several appeals had been made, I felt like there were needles being stuck in the back of the chair I was sitting on. I jumped up with my hand in the air, finding myself saying I would be willing to be Vice Chairman, if Peter would be Chairman. Peter looked flabbergasted, but not as much as I was — it was the correct decision, but what a way to make it!

It is true, if you wish to follow your true path, then *anything* can and will happen at *any time*, whatever we may think, or say otherwise. Needless to say, we enjoyed the work involved, which always consists of give and take, in any given job of office.

The NFSH, now vastly grown in numbers, is a body that is doing its best to safeguard people by making certain all healers are professional in their work and will be accepted by the medical profession as well as by other professional bodies. Therefore, the post offered to me as Training Officer enabled me to play a part in this, as well as organising talks and lectures, whereby one meets many of the varied professions, and many lovely people — Dennis Fare being one such person, a dedicated man who became Chairman of the World Federation of Healers, yet another body which is making great strides here and abroad to see that healers are of a high standard. He has since stepped down as Chairman. Peter became involved in its Council, representing Great Britain, with two other Council members, but that is another story.

Peter and myself now found we were out a lot more, lecturing and teaching. Committee, Council and AGM's took us to London and abroad; to Germany, Spain and other countries — we were now finding new outlets and friends that were to become important to the Centre in the future, though we did not see the full depth of it all, at the time.

We eventually stepped down from the positions mentioned above because we felt that we had done all that was possible in the circumstances that were given to us.

Since writing this chapter, the International Self Realization Healing Association (ISRHA) has come into being. I have become familiar with their beliefs and values, and have found ISRHA to be of the very highest standard, and well worth being part of.

The Name Self-Realization Healing Centre

That I had to wait, until the family were ready and able to accept this name, was true. The name Denton had been given to the Centre and because of this, it had to be respected before it could be relinquished.

Now the time had arrived, we agreed to remember and re-spect the name, but now, slowly, change it as Paramahansaji had wished, to the *Self-Realization Healing Centre.*

After once having changed the Centres name from Denton Healing Centre to Self Realization Healing Centre, which is what was asked of me, I then felt that it would have to remain with this name until I had built the Meditation courses up further, and, the time was fitting for a further change, so that this time the Centre would have its full complete name ~ never to change again.

This came about when it *was* time for the the Self Realization Healing Centre to become

The Self Realization *Meditation* Healing Centre

at last

complete in its entirety.

57

Christmas 1991

THE past year had been progressively busy, with little or no time for ourselves as a family; Christmas had arrived to give us a much needed rest.

Our Christmases are simple, whereby in great joy, we fast and meditate, going for walks and keeping a silence within and without, as much as it is possible. Special times come, for dancing, chanting, or talks of a spiritual nature, to uplift and help.

It was during the Christmas week that Ji Jesus came once more, to speak to me, to tell me that:

"The wind of great change is upon us all. Though the trees and branches will sway, roots uplift and destruction take place, I was to fear not, for we shall only feel the disruptive force… which we can change into constructive.

"Going with the will of life.
Speaking with the Holy Spirit.
It shall come to pass.

My words are Sacrosanct.

The Lamb of God, who takes away
The Sins of the World, has spoken.

Humble, I love and serve
all of life.
Aum."

To describe my feelings, on hearing these words spoken, in such a divine way, is beyond the realms of human ability. I bowed my head, realising that whenever a great Master finds reason to come and make themself known, it is because of great happenings ahead. I do not feel that I am worthy of such a visit from a Master... Ji Jesus.

There was still more beauty to come — not long after this visitation my loving Guru came to speak with me, his words came gently and firmly.

> "You have kept the silence for a long time, listen well my child of God. It is time for you to use your spiritual names, acknowledge all of them, but use only Mata Yogananda, for everyday purposes — I wish you to tell people your story... if they ask. You will never be accepted by those who know me in America; I have asked you to take on this task, knowing this, but knowing also, you have been born with this task in mind. Fear not, my love is with you."

His voice was so loving and tender that it brought tears to my eyes. He continued saying that there was more work to do outside the Centre now, and the relinquishment of the Centre to the family must soon be completed and that my time must be given completely to writing and strengthening my body, for the travels ahead of me —

> "I am well pleased with you, though there is much more to do yet *which will try your faith*. This responsibility that I now place on you, will affect the Centre and so you must pass on this message I give to you... to them.
>
> "In love I come.
> In love I go."

and with those last words, he left me to ponder on the words he had spoken.

Though I had been asked not to reveal my true identity, or him as my Guru, to any except the family, it is also true to say that this was not an easy thing to do, for when you love the Masters, you feel you want to shout it from the treetops. That I had the privilege of knowing and being taught by a Master Guru, only added to my ecstatic desire to shout his praises… now I was being allowed… at last… to come from my enforced silence… to do this first, and then do only the works that are asked of me — so help me God.

My final steps were now to be taken. Each time my thoughts had gone to the silly idea that my services were no longer being required, that there were no more mountains to climb, or ledges to rest upon, but each time another mountain was shown to me and yet again… more ledges to rest on the way.

I know that it is wrong to try to hasten our departure from this earth plane by our thoughts, and that by doing so, for whatever reason, would only cause us extra discomfort and pain.

For, as there is a time for *our arrival*, so there is a time for *our departure*, which is usually, and should be, when our 'blue print' for this life is finished… we have completed our task. Sometimes we are asked to stay and continue, if a task is so difficult that it can only be done by a certain person.

Though this is rarely the case, it does happen. Until then, we have a duty to live every second as the most precious second of all, accepting this with love and happiness… until called home by the *Infinite Beloved.*

I love you
I love you
I love you

58

Micheal's Progress

"WE do need office space Mataji."— I looked up from my bookwork and saw Micheal standing with a forlorn look on his face.

"You worked out and designed plans for a building Micheal," I said, "And the local council would not pass them, also you know we would need more money again".

"Yes, I do know this," he replied, "But not only do we need a larger office, but now a larger room for our courses."

Micheal had good ideas, but his love of spending money was great and a thing he had to balance out in his life; knowing this, I proceeded with caution.

"What are you suggesting?" I asked him.

"A different set of plans, making a two story building in place of the horse boxes in the courtyard." He answered.

My heart gave a leap, it sounded a good plan which Peter had mentioned to me a few weeks back, whereas the last one Micheal mentioned would have stuck out like a 'sore thumb' and would have had stairs going out of our bathroom — this was more practical; the other had been a folly to teach a lesson. This was, I felt, going to become reality. When the intuitive feeling is good, I believe it is there for us to act upon.

"If you design this Micheal and the plans pass the Council's inspection of them, then I will do my best to find some money."

No sooner were the words out of my mouth than he was out of the door and getting his drawing board up. Meanwhile, my thoughts were "money doesn't have a monopoly with anyone, there is plenty of it in the World… if it is meant, we should have this building, then the money will be found." And with this positive thought, I returned to my bookwork.

We waited with anticipation, only to find that not only the local Parish Council, but also the South Somerset County Council had turned the building application down. One Councillor, in particular, who lived nearby certainly had no liking for us and seemed to put every obstacle in our way, so much so that two members of the family wrote to the local parish magazine, and also stood up to the local Council with very strong words, as there was no good reason for their turning it down.

On the whole, the Council was a fair one, but as always, had its narrow minded members, or people who fear, because of their lack of knowledge of others people's professions. They did not realise how many people in Queen Camel were being helped by the healing, and Queen Camel itself, as well as the shops which were patronised by visitors to the Centre… till we *had* to tell them.

Following on from the refusal of our plans, a letter came from a man who had attended the Planning County Council hearing, he said he felt he could help us, so we asked him to come and see us. He introduced himself by saying he used to be in the Planning Department and had recently started up his own business helping people's appeals; he took on their cases if he felt that they should have had their applications passed. He continued by saying that our plans should have been approved, could he act for us? He was a fair man who would only accept a fee if he won his case, and he was certain that we would win, if we made an appeal.

Knowing it was no chance, that he was meant to act for us, and that it was time that the building should come into being and be built, the family gratefully accepted, while Christy took on all the paperwork that needed to be dealt with.

While this was happening, we had to make many journeys down to Bexhill, Sussex, where Peter's mother was in hospital. We knew she was not going to come out, but was preparing for her next journey. We saw her struggle to keep alive, yet she told us she wished to go and meet 'Pop' — Peter's father who passed many years ago.

"I believe she is staying alive, to see you," I said to Peter, "If you told her it's all right by you, for her to go, it might help her."

Peter is her only son and she loved him, above all else. The next time we went to see his mother, I left them to say their farewells, and by the following day she had 'packed up' and departed, to a further life of *no bodily pain.*

The last few hours of a person's life, on this earth plane, I do believe are very important, and they need to be left quietly to make their peace within *themselves,* which cannot be done while people sit there talking. People may think it is lack of love and care to leave them on their own, but to do so, and then explain to them the reasons, is I know, more caring and more loving in the end.

We attended Peter's mother's funeral, out of respect, knowing that the soul had already departed on another journey. We hastened back to the Centre as soon as possible afterwards, to continue our administration to the living. As everyone knows, there is a lot to do when someone passes and that the house must be cleared and cleaned. After several weeks, we had lovingly finished this task for Peter's mother, and now prayed that the house would sell fairly soon, as we were needed at the Centre.

It was not an easy time for selling houses, in fact houses were not selling at all, but lo, after several weeks, selling at a low price, we had a buyer and now our journeys to Bexhill could cease, knowing everything had been done, as she had wished.

On our return home we found, to our delight, that the appeal was going ahead and hopefully, would be passed. We would be able to start building with the money from the sale of the house, and hopefully the rest would follow later.

"Shall I help build the new building?" Micheal wanted to know.

"You have enough to do." I replied, "But we must start getting quotes from builders now, which I would like to leave in your hands, and if you will supervise the project, Peter and I can get on with our other commitments."

Micheal agreed to the idea, willingly.

As he agreed, I knew he would have a great deal more supervising to do than he was thinking, or intending to do, but he would see that it was all carried out properly. So having great respect for Micheal's abilities, I left the building of our new office and meeting room in his capable hands.

While all these plans were taking shape, and the family were working very hard, I had noticed the lack of exercise that they were able to take, due to the lack of time. They all loved swimming, but apart from the time factor, it was expensive for each of us to go regularly. They liked walking, but they did not have something for the complete body, to keep them healthy, as well as feeding the mental and spiritual part of themselves.

Christy and Daniel had already found out how therapeutic swimming and movement in the water could be, with children — not only teaching them how to overcome their fear of water, but also they observed how swimming gave them confidence in themselves and security in the water; others found it helped muscle problems or stiffness.

Seeing so many people benefitting from being taken to the swimming baths, and looking into and after their needs when there, I wondered what could be done! The next few days I could not get this thought out of my head.

I did not want this thought, it was a very *expensive* thought… get a swimming pool built in the garden… it was more than a thought by now, more like a pushing of an inner force to get it done.

Throwing out the idea as unnecessary, it would come back as necessary.

I threw it out of my mind each day, hoping I would find a reason for not having it… more building work… more noise… mess… too much money… but none of these thoughts helped, and

I intuitively knew by the deep feeling within me, that not only the family, but the patients young and old, would benefit from this project. I prayed long and hard that night to the Infinite Beloved, Father and Mother… and argued!

"But we already have a building being built and not sufficient money for it. How can this be happening so quickly? Please can I have a rest… for a little while… before this happens — and what about the money?"

I could hear the heavens and my beloved Guru laughing at me, and in their gentle laughter, the gentle words "Do my will… do life's will. You shall do this, for it is meant… go in faith and all will be well."

On my knees, I asked forgiveness for ever doubting the depth of my feelings that had been given to me.

Being all present and correct, the following morning at our meeting, I decided to put this idea to the family.

"How would you like a swimming pool?" I said

Thinking I was teasing them, one of them said, "We already have one in the courtyard."

Smiling to myself, I realised it was pretty true, it had been raining nonstop for a few days and we had one or two *grand* pools of water.

"We could have a covered swimming pool," I continued, "That it would be possible to use all the year — this way it would become a therapy pool and could be used as such."

Most thought it a wonderful idea, but Micheal was thoughtful and said, "It would have to be heated and be a large pool and have a good cover to withstand the wind and rain; therefore it will cost a lot of money."

"The money will no doubt have to be looked into, but first we will need to get an estimate." I replied, continuing to say that I felt it was a worthwhile idea, which would have to be done now as next year we would not have any time left for things such as these time consuming building projects.

Come

I spoke to them of their need to keep fit... enabling them to have abundant energy to give and help others, the importance of balanced energies which would only come about with balanced activities of the mind, body and spirit. They knew me well enough by now to know I would not do anything unless it was *meant to be* and in the plan of our lives.

So, having agreed in principle and with great enthusiasm and pleasure at the thought of future swimming, they left it to us to start 'the plan of action'.

I sent out a silent prayer for more money to be 'wafted' our way... please.

We did not have far to look for a swimming pool specialist — we wrote to several, but one approached us, a family concern, who would undertake to start the project immediately. Roger was his name, a likeable man, whom I felt we could trust to do his best. We asked him to build us a thirty three foot pool, with a heavy duty cover, no frills or fancies, but in the middle price range; with what we took to be a reasonable quote, the work commenced the following week.

Meanwhile, having found a builder that was sympathetic to our cause of developing and producing a two story building, without too much noise from the usual blaring radios and shouts of, "Tea up Jack", we left them with the knowledge that they had promised us a completed building within six months. There were the usual 'sticky situations' that always seem to apply with buildings, yet... up it was going... now I had to find more money before the six months was up. I did not have to ask — patients came to our rescue in donations of anything from five pence to hundreds of pounds. Slowly, we saved the thousands that were needed to pay for the completion.

We were so humbly grateful to all these people who saw our need and gave willingly, and the blessings to them, I know are many.

59

The Shower Room

THE swimming pool had to have supervision by one of the family and hereby lies another story of progress.

Micheal had taken on the responsibility of seeing everything was going according to plan. The pool was finished, the small shower room built, now all that was left to do, was build partitions separating the heater and mechanical parts from the changing room shower area.

The family were going through 'a growing' within themselves, and were a little 'tetchy' with each other. Micheal wanted to do the woodwork, not trusting anyone else to do it.

Daniel took a back seat feeling he could not do it.

Nini wanted to get into the garden.

Christy wanted to work with Daniel.

Knowing how clever life and the Infinite Power is, in solving these delicate problems — I left well alone, till one day about four o'clock I felt it was time for things to change. I instinctively put my hands over Micheal's and held them, knowing his work was finished and he must not proceed with any more.

Micheal had to retire with an unusual cold.

Daniel had to take over and do all the woodwork.

Nini had to help and not be in the garden.

Christy had to be in the kitchen, cooking.

From this, a hard lesson was given to all the family to progress from.

To show Micheal he was not indispensable.

Daniel, that he was capable of doing anything he had to.

That Nini had to be a servant and serve sometimes, and Christy's learning point, was that she could not be in on everything.

For myself, even now, wonderment of how life gives us the tests that we need, to help strengthen all our many weaknesses so that they become our strengths. When the family saw their mistakes, they were grateful for the lessons given to them. One could ask no more…

60

Love of Animals

W E were wondering what outlet our paddock, consisting of a quarter acre would eventually have.

I would love to have animals there, in abundance, feeding them, playing with them and we would *love* them all, but so far what it was to become had eluded us — so we waited.

We all loved animals and Daniel had a rapport with all of them, he would often be found with bees, spiders, mice, birds or slugs in the garden, watching them with interest. With the wounded animals, he knew instinctively what to do, alongside loving them. Thereby, quite naturally, as he was a Daniel, one who stands up *in* righteousness against all, so his second spiritual name became Francis, being courageous, yet gentle and loving, with great faith — he had truly become these two names.

Daniel Francis was not only a good healer, but an excellent counsellor, anything he took on himself to do, though apprehensive, he did well. His *love* and *faith* saw him through parts of life that he had not experienced, and with these two *essences,* he will never lack or want. My love for him, as for all of life, is deep and everlasting, and he, in his turn, reciprocates by doing the Infinite's will.

BBC TV approached us at about this time, asking us if they could come down to film the Centre with us healing animals.

"You can," I replied, once again asking them for a little time to arrange for animals to be here with their owners.

"Daniel, would you organise this with Christy?" I asked of him, "And both of you take the foreground this time and give the interviews." Peter and I needed to relinquish this role and it was now time.

"I would love to," he said, "And we will see if we can get some goats this time."

In no time at all, Daniel and Christy had lined up cats, dogs, goats and a rabbit that were in need of healing.

The rooms were made ready, one to put the cats in, dogs in another and the goats were in the paddock, with refreshments for those who wished it. Bowls of water or milk were available for the animals, with plenty of towels at the ready for whatever mishaps may take place.

This programme was going to be shown on *Country File,* we were informed by the four members of the TV crew who alighted with their equipment one sunny day. They had arrived late due to a hold up in traffic, but once here, everything was go–go–go. The smaller animals did not like the big arc lights on them, they can be very hot as well as producing an enormous amount of light, but apart from showing an eagerness to finish the whole thing, they played their part well.

Several people turned up with more animals than expected; one such person brought in a 'kid' goat which could not walk. Having given all the animals a healing under the arc lights, with the sun now shining brightly Daniel Francis took the kid into the garden and holding it in his arms, he put it gently down on the grass and oblivious to anyone, or anything, he put his hands out to heal — a few minutes later the kid shook itself, gave a small bleat and started to walk on its own away from Daniel. An interview followed, then the camera crew finished their filming, packed up and went on to their next assignment.

61

Progressive Help

WE were now settled in our new Centre with Micheal and Nini, two more of our spiritually chosen family, now much established with us.

In my progress all my knowings of what to do, or say, came to me from a depth of intuitiveness that I had acquired as the months and years had rolled by. This intuitiveness, at the depth that it was, could never fail me, less than that... would.

I knew now, that Micheal had a lesson to learn and that I, from his lesson, would at last, have my neck strengthened. I had put up with this weakness and pain knowing that it had a part to play in the future plan of things, but I am not ashamed to say, I was very pleased the time had come for it to be put right. My body was very sensitive to healing and Micheal was now to become my healer for a period of time, while he learnt 'fine adjusting' and also what to do if further professional help made itself known in the form of Chin Sen Lu.

The next few months were difficult for both of us; Micheal had to treat me as a patient, as well as Guru — which I was, in any given space. He did not know and was uncertain of how to react to this given situation; if he got himself lost in thought, was insensitive, or the slightest bit of ego crept into him at the time of his healing me, my body would suffer a temporary set back. His frustration was great, as he learnt through his mistakes. There were times when Chin Sen Lu would make himself known to me and work with Micheal, making him move his hands or take a step back. He would

265

sometimes move my arms so quickly, that Micheal narrowly missed getting many a cuff from the quickness of the unheeded movements.

One day, Micheal's frustration mounted — he asked me if I was the patient, or the Guru.

"I am the patient, with the Guru's tenderness," I said gently, knowing that it helped him to separate them, and yet, it was not necessary.

Micheal, being a good healer already, over the months soon became an excellent one and the time came when I knew he did not need to heal me any more. The exacting lesson and task had been completed.

Peter was to take over the strengthening process of my neck now, thereby allowing Micheal time to see more patients.

Chin Sen Lu thoroughly enjoyed himself and the three of us had many a good laugh 'to boot'.

62

Paperwork

CHRISTY had an enormous amount of advertising that I had asked her to take over from me, and with that, alongside her other work of healing, yoga and counselling, it was becoming too much for her.

She was a person who had learnt how to overcome any difficulties and did it with such peace and love, that she drew people to her unknowingly. She rightly earned the spiritual name of Little Mother, because she looked after everyone's welfare.

We had much paperwork to do before, and on moving to Queen Camel we had even more of which Christy, 'Little Mother', did most. If it is organising, teaching, cooking or paperwork — whatever comes her way, Christy never minds, but does it with love. Her writing and advertising material are, needless to say, first class.

"Could we afford to have someone to help on the office side?" Christy asked.

"Not really" I replied, "On the other hand, we can't afford our 'Little Mother' being ill."

"I know someone who would be very good."

"Who is that?"

"Someone who already knows us, called Alex, who used to work in publicity in a big way."

"She may want a big wage," I replied, "And that we can't afford, but let us have a talk with her."

Alex was a person with a fine mind, who was now in need of work to help her financially with the upkeep of her children and herself.

"Would you like to come and work with us?" I asked.

"Oh, I would, very much." She replied.

"We need someone who will work with the family and do whatever is needed."

"I do not mind what I do."

"Do you mind ironing and washing up?"

"Not if you need me to do it." was her reply.

Next, we had to talk about money — there was no difficulty as she would accept what we could afford. Her desire within, to progress, to find peace and Self-Realization, were only too evident.

I do not believe, at that time, she was aware of how 'hungry' she was for this and much more, I only knew that she was to become an important member of the family.

Steve, was her partner and they both represented what is a truly spiritual partnership — it would have its firing in the kiln of their hearts and the results will be edifying to all around them.

So yet another came.

Meanwhile, the garden was, unfortunately, getting neglected. No time at present for weeding, seeding or pruning. To see us through this patch, we enlisted the help of a gardener, called Paul who helped to get the garden into shape — he stayed a while, to reap here as he sowed, but one day he had to go his way to sow and reap elsewhere, but before he left he did leave the garden in a manageable state.

Many people were offering their help to us now, be it in part payment for a course, or just for love of helping us. These people are important to us, whoever comes is family to us and can only be separated in their own mind by their thinking process. Nothing gives us greater joy than to see and have 'whomever', work with us, eat with us and pray with us — *if they wish to.*

It is by giving that we receive.

And, if only everyone that had a problem no matter what it is… could do this and give with caring, or love, then they would find their minds occupied and their hearts glad, and by this process in itself, they would find the peace they are seeking. Too many people, with sickness of the mind or body, go *in on themselves,* and create more havoc with more nervous tension and pain, than is ever necessary.

I say this in full knowledge that what is being written is not that easy to do and often needs a 'helping hand' from someone else, to begin the recuperation period.

Much of our work is voluntary, consisting of home visits or talks for which we do not always ask payment, even for the petrol. Some patients need to receive only and not give — that is for a short while, until they feel strengthened and want to give. I remember only too well such a time when I was empty — there was just a 'void'… that needed filling. I had *nothing* to give — nowhere or no-one to go to — In this state I was found and 'given to' — for a long time I drank and ate everything given to me, of kindness, caring, peace and rest until one day I became whole again, finding myself at last, I could and wanted to, give. I shall never forget that time and that is why *everyone* must have what they *need* at this Centre.

Love
is
Contagious

63

Names and Blessings

THERE is a saying 'he lived up to his name', it could also have been 'down' to his name. Let me explain — we all get given a name when we are born. The father and mother pick a family name, or a name of perhaps a film or recording artist whom they have long admired — for better or for worse. Maybe this name does suit us, our personality and character for a few years to come, but what about as we change within ourselves and strive to become better human beings… what happens then? It has been scientifically proved that there is energy in *everything* — if this is so, then there must be energy in our breath as we speak, what we speak about, and likewise, in the words that we speak. Each letter has its own light and shade, so each name, made of these letters, also has its quantity of light and shade.

As we grow, not so much in age, but *inwardly*, people can feel uncomfortable with their 'birth name' and try to live with it, instead of trying to think of how *not* to live with it. Nowadays, it is easier for people to change these names, but why change it unless you have some name worthwhile changing it to? — that is unless you get a deep inner feeling about a specific name you should change it to. In which case, go ahead and change it, otherwise, it must be left 'till we grow into another one, or if treading the spiritual path of life, you find a spiritual guide, or Guru, who can see with their 'eye' and find the one name you need, perhaps, to last you most of the rest of your mortal life.

Along with names what about blessings?

"We do not need blessings of any kind from anyone" — so often these words are said by someone, without knowing the truth, or having the knowledge of such matters. Blessings could be given by anyone, to anything, but what good would it do? — For example, if you were blessed by a criminal, how much light would he have in his words... not much, perhaps mostly shade, no light or colour to uplift you higher in your own *now* light.

So, we have variations on a theme, the more love and less ego we have, the better the blessing will be; names and blessings are important, always, to some degree. However, in the right God given hands, it can start changing your whole life.

An example of this is of my own name, given at birth, Judy — it was given to me, because mother expected another boy; a baby girl took her by surprise and it was the first name to find its way to her lips. As Judy, I was a 'tomboy', and I changed my name when it had been superfluous for a long time; I then became Rena, *because I had changed,* and later on, my Guru bestowed on me my spiritu-ally given names, as I grew once more, *within myself,* — these are now the *chosen* ones, for the rest of my life on this earth plane.

64

Yogananda Room

BEING a busy Centre, with all of us having our respective work to do, we hardly ever had the whole family together, unless it was at meditation time, or in the morning at 8.30 for our meetings — so any decisions would be held over for these times, if possible.

One such time I suggested we should call our new building the 'Yogananda' room, for that was one of my Guru's names, as well as being one of mine.

It means 'one in bliss' — yoga (one) ananda (bliss).

We were going to use the large ground floor room for yoga, meditation and other spiritual disciplines.

"What do you think, family?" I asked.

After a few moments thought, they agreed it would be a lovely name — so that was decided upon.

*Where there are
Master Gurus
There is always untold Wisdom*

65

Our Relationships

MY time with our family, now growing steadily larger, had been one of complete happiness within, though having to chastise them at times. My love for them all became even greater as this had to be done.

When Daniel was with me, we would go out to the coast or woods together; now when the time permitted, I tried to find time to go out with each member of our family, when we could walk, or talk, allowing time for them to get to know me as a person, as well as a Guru, all the time knowing full well that it was very difficult for them to see and accept me on all these different levels.

They were becoming more aware of the family as a wider ever expanding unit, each working individually, yet together, to reach a state of Self-Realization and unconditional love which the Centre, and all those in it, and visiting it, thrived on. One day, I knew without doubt, intuitively, that I was now being asked to relinquish all we had built up; as this came to me I felt a sudden shift of energies within my body, as if my body knew the bulk of my work had been done and it could now release and take a further rest. To do this, I knew we had to go away more, to make the family more reliant on themselves and not on me or Peter.

Peter and I had many commitments outside the Centre, so whenever we felt the need… for the family's sake, we would find something to do away from the Centre and go… always on our return we found progress, from disruption within themselves that had taken place and then been rectified.

Only now am I allowed to reveal the full facts, to allow the readers to see how the family and Centre had grown.

Now, having been given the right to release everything, we slowly gave each member of the family more responsibility, with the shopping, the running of the house, the Centre and finally, when they had all seen the art of balancing accounts, whether in the red or not, the receipts and bills were given to them.

ONE learns and knows how best *TO DO*
At this time of life that is.
But to give, see, look, but not *TO DO,* is an art
worth pursuing.

66

Thoughts

*H*OW many more Easters we shall spend together, I do not know.

Easter time was upon us again and we had a silent retreat — many people came, to be with us. This retreat consisted of complete silence, dispersed with several spiritual talks. Light buffet meals were set out for people to choose whether they fast or not. The meditation room was there, open day and night for those who wished to use it, and the surrounding countryside awaited them, with walks. One member of the family was always on duty, for anyone to break the silence and empty their hearts to, if they felt the need. For, at these special retreats, progress would come through the emptying of dross and the refilling with peace.

I looked for and found Micheal and Nini, on the Easter Monday morning, when the retreat had finished. I had something to ask them.

We had a blessing of a six months old baby taking place at 3.30pm at the Centre. Before this I wished to bless the names that were ready to be given to the family.

"Would you help me with the ceremony for Christy and Daniel." I asked of them, "We will need pure water in a bowl, some form of fire, or heat and oil, with appropriate flowers around the Yogananda room." I hastened to add that Christy and Daniel did not know of the ceremony as I wished it to be a loving surprise for them.

"They will be going for a short walk fairly soon, we will get the room ready then," said Micheal and Nini.

We went into the Yogananda room and the whole family came and sat in a half circle... including our three dogs.

I, as their Guru, to my devoted disciples, fired, cleansed their old names away and blessed their new ones. Then as a surprise to the other members of the family, Peter received his name of Sevananda (Service in bliss to others). Micheal took his second name John (Gift of God) and Nini Dovananda (Peace and bliss). These latter given names were given so that they could aspire to them.

We then celebrated with sun-kissed pure water and sweet-meats.

We had shared a very important ceremony of blessing and giving the family their spiritual names, which was a long awaited dream come true, for me.

67

Character Differences

MOST families have at least one child in it that is different, in quite a drastic way, from the others, but in ours there was no difference, except for the fact that *every* member of the family was completely different in character, personality and abilities.

I believe we choose the womb and the family that we wish to be born into, the one that will usually present the problems that *we* need to overcome, then we have perhaps what is called a 'blood relationship' to that family. We sometimes feel tied by this relationship, and feel a moral obligation to understand, respect and help them, if possible.

However, bearing in mind that we need a womb to nourish ourselves in while seeds, and someone to help us through our tender years, plus the fact that there had to be a *physical* act, brought about by a man and woman, to bring our life energy back into being as a baby, then I would say there must be an arrangement made at a higher level for all this to happen, even if the seed is only in the 'womb' for a little while. *This has to happen,* so how much better, if afterwards, our families can become close friends, with no ties to bind us, only that of love and understanding — *then* we can *grow.* A different generation must draw away to progress. To stay in and with the older generation, at all times, steals our progress from us.

We then marry and start our own family and the cycle of life continues, or we find a link with a group of people — now that we are old enough in ourselves, to make a change for the better within. We can 'mix and match' becoming part of a group, without losing our identity, or our freedom. This is what happened at this Centre. A gathering of like minds, waiting to share, give and receive, yes, there is a spiritual *head*, but only until each is wise unto themselves, then each will listen to the other, and the one with the most wisdom at that given moment of time will be listened to, by the other members of the family. No criticism, or judging each other, only understanding and allowing for each others imperfections — with love.

Being different adds 'spice' to a family and makes each member look to themselves. Christy and Daniel have been written about and are more introverts, Micheal and Nini are more outgoing.

Nini, has a quick mind, a talent for writing articles and drawing, a good sense of humour and a good mimic of bird calls — she is a precise person. Micheal loves rock climbing and pursuits of a demanding nature — he has many varied talents, as written about and he is a more 'laid back' person.

Peter always has got a smile on his face — he keeps us all smiling, as well as earthed. His gentleness and yet strength of healing and counselling have been well known, for many years.

As for myself, I cannot speak, and leave it to the reader to come to their own conclusions.

I do know, and have been told by my Paramguru, Swami Sri Yukteswarji, that this is the way forward. If family groups can be formed by love and wanting to give, and not by any lack of security or wanting to opt out of life, then the whole world would soon reap the benefits. But, this will be a slow process... to be worked towards, likened to the seed of a tree that takes hundreds of years to grow tall and strong, to become beautiful, giving shade under its leaves in the hot sun, and shelter from the rains that fall.

BUT IT WILL HAPPEN

68

Resignations

"**P**ETER, it's time to resign from the NFSH." I heard myself saying one day. "We must give up our positions, for we have other things that must be done — and done now."

"Yes," Peter replied, "I have felt this for several weeks now." Members we would remain, but the feeling of 'new pastures' was very strong within us both.

Peter's father had been Chairman of the NFSH a long time ago and he and Peter had watched it grow from small beginnings. It was now a sizeable organisation, but we had travelling to do. My book, and other writings, had to be written soon, at sometime in the near future, so we passed the job of Chairman and Vice Chairman over, so that younger blood could take it forward still further.

Have you ever noticed that what you feel you are not good at, or cannot do, you *virtually get given,* and surprisingly find it can be done very well; this is just one paradox of life, with all dualities running alongside it. Problems, and taking up new pursuits, are so *important* to our growth — each time a new one comes along and we accept it, even if not perfectly done, we find we get given a strength within, and this is how we build to become strong people.

Our resting time is when there are no problems
Our progressive time is when we have *one* or *more*
We need both to get a perfect balance.

*When we do the least
we do the most*

69

Truth

To hear people say that they always speak the complete *truth* is not something to be admired in a person, but not to speak *untruths* is. Sometimes one has to be 'cruel to be kind' — good surgery work, but this should only be done if 'needs be' and done in love, otherwise a very tender scar is left.

A person can only take so much truth at a given time, sometimes more than they think they can take, but *less* than you may give them. We have to judge correctly, or say nothing — how do we get, or find the balance?... well ... become an *egoless* being, this will ensure that the words we utter come from the correct depth of ourselves, at the right time, but they have to be uttered with the strength and knowledge that they are needed and *correct* — it is a large responsibility. After the words have been said, and if they are spoken as they should be, the return result will vary with all the levels of emotions in each person. Great strength is needed to deal with *truth*.

As a spiritual teacher will know, you can only give the truth to your students on the level that they can develop from, often not appreciating what you say, even defying you, which is their right. The responsibility then, is for the teacher to stand back in love, and wait... patiently.

Through my lifetime, in this capacity, I can never be my true self, for people could not relate, *likewise*, to divulge truths that sound false to the ears of mankind would be disastrous to the complete structure of life, so the best is done, and as we all reach different evolutionary states, so will *truth* unfold to more *truth*.

A small example, in a human way, is when Joyce and Harold wished to help us financially, but only if we would not mention their names — how difficult this was to do… when you cannot tell even your own family the complete truth… and they must trust your words without full knowledge of the situation — yes, it is difficult. Another instance, is when you see in your minds eye the end result of a problem involving someone else, but *must not* divulge, or take part in that problem — you are only allowed to stand and watch the act.

This is difficult, until you *know* and *feel* at one with the Universe and understand that progress comes from pain and loss as well as from happiness, the latter is more often than not, a said resting state.

70

How the Divine Masters Work

EACH stage of evolution, as we know, brings us a different criterion and likewise we need different people, with different ideas to project us forward into this new era.

Guru is a much maligned word in this day and age; there seem to be gurus for baked beans, washing up liquid and anything else one likes to name. The people that use this name so loosely, are obviously ignorant of its importance, or do not believe there is such a word appertaining to certain persons… more fool them.

There are many self–made Gurus whom on reading books, or with a little teaching, feel that they can take on that role. No, they cannot — it must be given… it cannot be taken. Those that take it upon themselves are the dangerous ones, then the saying 'a little knowledge does a lot of harm' comes into its truth.

True Gurus like Paramahansaji are people who have unconditional love for all God's creatures — wisdom and peace are the attributes alongside this; they are very strong beings in their faith and spoken words. Never unjust, yet quite able to scare and put an unwanted quick tongue into silence. Their job is dispelling darkness, which means bringing knowledge to dispel fear which in its turn dispels ignorance. They are skilful surgeons who will cut away the 'dross' with love and then heal the wound with careful thought.

Come

They can read your mind, if they wish, but will not invade your privacy unless it is necessary. Knowing the devotee completely, and having insight into *all*, it is not wise to try to pull the wool over their 'eye'.

If there is any ego, selfishness, pride or such like left within a person, then that person could not be a true Guru — this is how we know them, *not* by their name, but *'by their deeds are they known'*.

Never give up on finding some much wiser person, if you are in need they will come, but in their own time, *not* ours. They are of all creeds and religions, yet of none. No dogma, only truth reigns within — as their words are spoken, many fall by the wayside, for future fruition; other seeds get taken and absorbed by minds that are ready, but so few can read the great depth that is within each spoken word that is uttered.

This is just a little about Gurus and Masters, much more can be explained by reading *Autobiography of a Yogi* which goes into detail on such matters.

71

A Cottage with a View

ON one of my usual walks down a leafy lane, on my way to see the donkeys and the horses that were in a nearby field, I felt this part of my life was coming to an end and another one beginning. Taking only slight notice of these thoughts, I called to the donkeys and looked to see if the horses were in the field. One small, frail donkey was already sniffing my hand — another came to push him out of the way to take the grass I had to offer.

As we conversed, with our thoughts of vibrating energy, there was a silent voice within that spoke, saying "Come, we have to talk." I did not recognise the feel of the voice, but stopped my 'chat' with the donkeys and walked on.

"Time to write your book now, and as you will not be able to write it here..." I interrupted saying, "Why not?"

"How many times does a knock come on the door? And how often are you needed downstairs, with the family, or for the patients?" The gentle voice continued. "Find a cottage, with a view, away from the crowd and write your book, you will be helped."

The excitement within me was mounting now as I thought of the many questions I wished to ask on this topic!

"But, my life story will not be of any interest"... I was thinking... an instant reply came:

"You are mistaken."

"But my Guru's book, that he wrote, is so good and lacks nothing — I could not write like that."

"All people write for different reasons, it makes them no lesser or greater — nor their books."

"I am not a writer and as for my spelling… I am not worthy of the task…" My feeling of confusion, that had taken over from the excitement was due to the many negative thoughts that were now besetting me.

The gentle inward voice continued "It is for *you* to do this given task" — he continued saying, "The writings must be about your life, not only of the suffering, but also the joys and of your journey through life to Self–Realization". As he stopped, my thoughts were of how already the 'impossible' had been done… many times over, in my life, so *why* was I doubting now?

I hung my head in shame, with this great realisation and asked forgiveness.

"Yes, I will do this — the book will be written… with God's helping hand."

On my return I asked Peter, "Will you help me find a cottage in the country, somewhere very quiet, with a view, which does not cost the earth and has every amenity to help us in our work?"

"You don't want much." He replied jokingly, at the same time, asking what it was for.

"For writing a book." I said and continued, "Will you type while I write?"

By now, Peter, knowing me as his wife and Guru, sensed the importance of what I was saying and he agreed to help in whatever way he could. I went on to tell him of the conversation that had taken place and as I spoke I saw with clarity, the whole project.

"I need complete *carte blanche* — would you be prepared to cook and type the manuscript for a few weeks, while I write this book that has been asked of me, lovingly… and you will need an electric typewriter." I added. There was no hesitation in Peter's reply.

"Of course, I will, let us start to look straight away."

As with most happenings that come at the *right* time, it only took Peter and myself a short while to find the very cottage. Four weeks from the date of finding it, we travelled down there and found everything we needed — it was a perfect setting with weather to match. Our hosts and owners of this lovely farm are known as Carol and Bernard, two most caring and kindly people to whom nothing was too much trouble.

The cottage was set in some three hundred acres of pasture land, with many varied trees and ponds as my viewpoint; there were sheep and cattle grazing, fish somersaulting in the ponds, and ducks making their flights during the day, with the changing colours of the gorse and trees and grasses of ever–changing hue. With all this in front of me, while writing, it was the perfect setting. Meanwhile the cottage had all facilities and was not too far from the coast in Corn-wall.

In this setting the book was written.

On awaking the first day, we indulged ourselves with perusing the area and getting some sea air into our lungs. The second day it was time for work.

As I sat, after having had our meditation and a light breakfast, my pen poised… I waited for a feeling to commence… like waiting for a 'pistol' to fire, or a one… two… three… *GO;* feeling none of these starting points, I tried to start writing. Living, as I had been taught, in the moment of time, with no past or present in mind, I now found it difficult to recall my past life, back to the memory level, in fact, did I want to? — No… but I must do so and truthfully, as it felt to me at that time, with no deception in my thoughts being allowed.

As the days flew by, I knew help was being given to me and that the writings were being changed by me, yet *also* by my co–writer called 'Master', who I was very aware of being present in my thoughts if I took a wrong turn; or if I got into difficulty of any kind while I was writing, the adviser was there. Otherwise, I got on with my 'scribble' and Peter with his dual role of cook and secretary.

While writing this book I also knew there were to be more books to come — one of stories and poems and one on Self–Realization through Meditation and so allowing the flow to come and go as it wished, we got used to this new pattern in our lives, with new thoughts and knowledge of the past and future now being acquired more rapidly as I progressed with the book. — It took those four weeks plus six more to finish the written copy.

During the last six weeks my body became ill and once more I wondered how long my body could contain me. It was a good body, that had housed me well, but now it felt very tired and my longing for its freedom, longing also for my spirit to be free, was heavy upon me. After all, the family had become of age and could cope well now; Peter, though knowing of his deep love and understanding was a self–sufficient person, as we all *should* be, so why NOT... I thought on... with my work done, could I get 'on the train again', this time home, to my Infinite Beloved... light and love.

Surely, there must be work to do there I reasoned, though with the knowledge that I had, I did not wish to rest on other planes while many are lost and suffering. I had hoped to return as quickly as possible, to this earth plane and continue working at whatever level was needed of me, but in a different body.

Since then, knowledge that this is not to be, and that my work must be continued elsewhere, when my time comes to pass, made me ask that I may help as many souls as possible now — at least... to sow seeds that will germinate in this lifetime, or another. I have been granted this request and with this knowledge, I rest my case.

> We all help everyone, sometime and somewhere
> In everything we learn something.
> Between everyone there is an exchange of energy
> and progress, be it from their laughter or bitterness.

Life will go on and forward, whatever *we* do. Sometimes we are granted permission to help souls as opposed to bodies and minds — we are not allowed the privilege unless we are egoless and ageless, but then evolution moves on.

We all choose our parents and my choice of parents, in retrospect, has given me all that was needed to start me off on my path in life.

There are no regrets… for my path was mapped out well, by a 'master map maker'.

My higher Self knows what is needed in this *one* span of life, and it knows what this *one facet* of myself is destined for — as *your* higher self will know.

A curtain *must* be drawn over our past lives, otherwise this life could become impossible to live in.

BE IN IT, NOT OF IT and it will be, but cannot hurt you.

Having not asked, but nevertheless been shown my past life, because of the need to see my capabilities, it became clear to me also, the great responsibility one takes on oneself with this given knowledge. It is not given lightly, for you have to be strong enough to accept whatever is shown to you, the bad as well as the good. We could become big headed or despondent, depending on our character… this would not do… therefore, it is wrong to seek our *past* or our *future*, but if it comes through need, for whatever the reason, we must be able to accept and continue in life as we had done up to that moment in time. This is why it is *not given lightly*. Furthermore, it must be truth from a *much higher level* and not make–believe — as it so often can happen that way.

Being a person who can only teach by experience and not 'hearsay', because the need to know that which I teach is the truth of this moment, my recall on the experience level had to be… and could only be, by experiencing life… not reading about it. The re-maining, that I did not need to experience for this lifetime, I was shown how to recall… only when needed… with my 'mind's eye', or given by my Guru.

The truth, and therefore the beauty of that which is being writ-ten, is that it shows we do *not* have to search for *anything* — we only have to need it (not want it), and our desire and the *need* will activate the positive energies around us, to bring this *need* into func-tion. Our paths are many and varied.

If you think about a beautiful diamond with its many facets, each facet reflecting beauty of a different *nature*, then look and see… we are like a diamond, each facet reflecting beauty of a kind… a different life… to each facet.

If we do well with the 'facet of life' in this lifetime, be it whatever we work at, then that facet will shine with truth and beauty. To complete all facets and make a *perfect* diamond, we have to have experience of many lifetimes, not necessarily on this earth's plane, but *somewhere,* to achieve this. The experiences have to be on every level, with our imperfections becoming our perfections, and as this happens, with our *exit and return* we become perfected Light and enter the realm of light, yet able to come and go as we wish with perfect liberty and love.

A day. A night. A dream, of a large rambling house set in rustic surrounds without a single blemish of the spirit found by the desire, fed by love and positivity and kept alive with more spirit. Why do the birds sing, the flowers grow tall? — Because this is the ground of a growing family group, called the Alpha–Omega, destined to prosper with the love of God within them.

The Alpha–Omega family must be of unconditional love, each and everyone with high intuitiveness and the ability to change direction at any given time without an imbalance of any one thought during the process.

It must be unjudgemental and at the very highest in complete harmony with all of nature.

SELF ~ REALIZED ~ GOD

72

Stepping Stones

*L*IFE will always have its problems, these we see as good
stepping stones.

Joy, peace and unconditional love has never left me since
finding my own Guru — spiritual guide — to all that is good and
need in this lifetime. I know that Peter Sevananda feels the same.

Just because people are ignorant of what a Guru truly is —it
does not mean the whole world has to be so ignorant — and even
deny their existence, does it?

Is it ignorance, from fear or pride that makes this happen? Or
just through trying to be funny? Either way,

don't let it happen to you.

Many times myself and others have been asked by people —
how are they to know — *what* Meditation is it that we teach here.
Is it T.M.?[22] I could see that this was causing concern in many
differrent ways and that it needed to be recified. Any descriptive
name given to Meditation would *box it in*, so the name had to be
one that no–one could *box* or *tie up*.

Pure came to me one night after Meditation — as being
the only suitable word for expansion, and to capture the deepest
essence of the Meditation, so came the added name of
Pure Meditation

73

Spiritual Partners

*A*S two people are brought together to do God's work ~ *needs* of others come before our own ~ either individually or collectively. This way we know *'all will be well'* ~ or in other words as *'God Wills.'*

We have different parts to *play* in life, so, our thinking and actions are trained into individual roles, which can take us apart from each other for many hours or days. Silence may be needed - inhibiting talk. Sometimes it needs only one of us ~ other times both of us **'on the job'**.

Either way our love, respect, faith in each other and above all our work for all of life is *paramount*.

74

A Young Devotee

THERE was a young devotee working at a Self Realization Meditation Healing Centre who felt that it would soon be time to leave. Being of devotion and faith in God and Guru, they checked with me to see if this was so.

I said, "Do you feel it is right away?"

"No" was the answer.

"Wait a while" I said, "While you allow this feeling to get stronger or weaker." I knew that the thinking was correct on *this* side, but, allowing there is no set time in spiritual awareness, a true thought will present itself quite often to prepare us for what will happen in the time ahead. More often than not this happens, so we have to have this awareness with patience so that we do not pre-empt, but, find intuitively the correct 'timing' and place for any given event in out daily lives. *Then* all will benefit.

This person waited until a further, deep feeling came ~ once more we spoke, once more it was not time.

Evidently the correct time came for the best outcome ~ I knew this and so did the devotee. They left to continue doing God's work, and found their next step before the final one, that now encapsulates all their dreams.

Such is inner feeling and higher intuition coupled together with faith and devotion to God/Guru and wanting what is right.

Some do not leave a Centre like this and live to regret it ~ for they are using ego and pride and want ~ not the Higher Wisdom of themselves.

So this is the final story of a strong inner feeling that Peter Sevananda and myself were to travel ~ patience to wait for the correct time, then, faith to go without full knowledge of the *why,* until much later in this story, of how we can always be guided if we go in faith wanting only the best to prevail for all concerned.

We write for this reason only ~ so that it may help others to see more clearly how the inner feeling of the

Higher Self's Intuitiveness

can work for YOU

75

Going Forward

MUCH was happening at the Mother Centre in the UK. People coming, going, or just passing through, advancement on all levels taking place.

So it was that we started our journeying (Peter Sevananda had frequently stated that he felt we would be travelling abroad soon:- my answer to that was always "God's Will be done".) Soon it was apparent to both of us that it was time to leave the Mother Centre in the care of the Alpha~Omega family's capable hands, while we visited our blood daughter in Australia, whom we had not seen for many years.

Linda had been taught Pure Meditation by myself whilst on her 'sojourn' in the U.K., her loving nature and the desire to help people brought her into the field of healing. She had a partner who was a courier by trade and whom we had not yet met.

On our arrival via Hong Kong at Sydney airport the reunion was one of love and joy. Being a long journey, after catching up with the past news, we needed to rest, which we did at their home in Rose Bay on the outskirts of Sydney.

76

Paddington

*A*S we travelled around I felt intuitively that the time had come for us to look at the property market. Acting on intuition without full conscious knowledge of why this had to be done, we started making enquiries and taking notice of sale boards that were around that area. Eventually we felt the need to look further afield to which Linda and her partner offered to take us around. On final realization that we were meant to look towards this property being a Sister Centre we started looking in earnest for the requirement that would be needed for such a Centre. 'But who to run it?' — This was a problem that I dared not think about at the time. I simply *had* to go in faith. On a visit to Paddington a suitable house was brought into our view. The house had three storeys in excellent condition and was very central to all amenities.

This was it, no doubts in our mind. Still I had to push back the penetrating thought of who was to run this Centre, for surely it could not be for myself or Peter Sevananda to stay and run it. Pushing back the thoughts once more, knowing this to be the chosen house we proceeded with the purchase. By now our time was very limited and there was no time for delay.

On our return to Rose Bay, Linda asked to have a word in private with us, stating that she would like to be considered as a potential person to run the Centre in Paddington. The Infinite works in unusual ways ~ here was the answer. Though Linda's partner was not knowledgbable in the Centres' working he was however very happy with the situation and said he would be supportive. It was Linda, though, having the necessary qualifications, alongside her abundant love for all, who would be fully in charge and respon- sible for the running of Paddington as a Sister Centre.

We were aware that we would have to return several times to Australia to help to organise and teach courses. For, once Linda and her partner had taken up residence in the Centre, there were the tasks of furnishing it to attend to, and the organising of printed matter, including brochures for advertising the Centre, to name but a few. This would be the priority on our next visit.

77

New Zealand

NEW Zealand was our next port of call, visiting two devotees who had started their own Centre up at Leigh in the North Island. We also took the opportunity of meeting many more like–minded souls.

We had known Deb and Laugharn for some time, having met them in the UK. Deb worked in the TV Media, and had come to us as an agnostic to sample a healing and request an interview which she wished to tape. I did not mind this at all and entered into her confrontational attitude with the full knowledge that all would go to the Divine plan. On her leaving I wondered if we would ever meet again. A few days later there was a phonecall saying that the tape had not recorded, there seemed to be no fault with the recorder could she come again?

After these two meetings Deb came regularly not only to see myself but also to take a course in Pure Meditation and Natural Spiritual Healing. While this was happening she introduced her partner Laugharn to the Centre who also became interested in all courses and decided to take them herself. It was not long after that they decided to emigrate to New Zealand to start their own Centre.

On our arrival our first port of call was in Auckland; we then decided to hire a car for the remainder of our stay to help us with the commitments of travel.

Leigh is approximately a two hour journey from Auckland. It was our delight to find the Centre in a beautiful area, near to the sea, with a small harbour and coastal walks. Our days were full, meeting people who were in need of spiritual advice and upliftment.

We were made truly welcome by Laugharn with her loving nature and with Debs zest for life they had created a very warm and welcoming place for people to imbibe and have healings. After several days it was time to wend our way further up the coast. visiting such places as Maugaturato, Whangarei, Opua, and Kaeo continuing on until we felt we had gone as far as we should. This journey, that we knew we had to make, was very interesting in more ways than one. We wished to meet more people of the Maori race, which we did, including a very important personage at the Waitanga Meeting House. On entering the house I felt a very strong presence, it was so strong and so 'needy' that I inwardly started asking if there could be peace and love between the peoples and if there was a message for the West.

I did not truly expect an answer or anything else in return, when suddenly, a forceful loving presence made itself known to me and in no uncertain terms I heard inwardly a reply to my question. It was:

"You come in peace and love. Many come with destruction in their hearts, destroy the forests and take land, and will be destroyed by their own thinking. The trees and land must be respected, go in peace and goodwill."

Then there was a further saying in Maori tongue that I did not understand. What I did know, though, was that these people need so much more understanding and love given to them, for, how little we all understand other peoples and their ways of life. This Maori Chieftain did speak further to me on Maori matters concerning myself and what his wish was that he wanted me to do ~ to help. This I cannot write of now, but if you look carefully you will see a happening of events between Maori and Pakaha that will stem from this very important meeting and conversation.

Bearing in mind the long distances between places, and the wish to see as much of the North Island as possible so that we may get a more rounded idea of the peoples and their ways of life, we covered much ground. For this surely, I know, will come into the context of the Mother Centre in the future.

This was a fact-finding mission and I feel that we traversed most of the North Island and had enough knowledge to let the Divine Plan proceed.

78

Malaysia

*A*LWAYS letting our intuition guide us, we knew on our next visit to Australia that we needed to make a stopover in Malaysia hoping for a possible few days rest, though, we knew full well that there must be a deeper reason in undertaking this part of Asia.

Having landed at Penang airport we made our way to our hotel where we quickly unpacked and had a look round before dinner. On the following day knowing that the area was well known for its lovely dressmaking materials, we asked to be taken to one of the major manufacturers not only to see them being made, but to buy some materials for the Alpha-Omega family. Each length needed to be intuitively chosen, with the colours that each of the family members needed which would be for their present *state* of being, or **state** to be.

Colours are so very important, not only to the wearer, but also to the *eye* of the beholder.

Continuing on our way, chauffeured by a young Malaysian man whose name was Falze (he being our original driver from the airport to the hotel) we stopped in Penang itself to have lunch and buy further material for myself, with which Falze helped us strike a bargain and proved to be invaluable in helping us to find a good place to eat and good sights to see. Our sightseeing included a typical colourful Chinese Temple, but what we really wanted was to visit a Mosque, which Falze took us to whilst he explained to us in his broken English that taking photographs would be frowned upon.

We went in to the Mosque, removing our shoes, myself putting a scarf over my head out of respect. The Mosque was virtually empty, with only one old man just sitting against a pillar who nodded as we passed him. We were impressed with the peaceful atmosphere. We said a prayer and came out. On our rejoining Falze he mentioned it was unusual for Europeans to be interested in visiting a Mosque and showing the respect that we did. *More questions came from him.*

We were pleasantly surprised to see Falze turn up one evening at our hotel wishing to ask further questions about ourselves and our work, and then asked us if we would like to see photographs of his family. This we understood later was a privilege given only to accepted friends.

We now felt it was time to rent a self-drive car to take us to Kuala Lumpur ~ visiting selected areas en route.

The Malaysian people were very kind and hospitable, shy, perhaps waiting to see our approach to them. If they are approached with respect and kindness then we found they would reciprocate.

Our rental car was of Malaysian make and not very comfortable, but at least it had four wheels and went!

On our way back to Kuala Lumpur we passed through Ipoh. I felt a strange excitement within me, it was as if this area could become important to us, in what way I did not know, but felt contented to let that feeling grow or subside.

The heat of Malaysia was getting through to us. That and our uncomfortable car made us very appreciative of our hotel on our arrival at Kuala Lumpur.

We found through our many enquiries in the areas visited that spiritual healing and Pure Meditation were comparatively unknown, but people had shown some interest and we felt that there was a need of further knowledge and enlightenment.

We were not long at Kuala Lumpur, but, the time we had was spent seeking out people and what they knew of our work. I wanted very much to see or hear more about Ipoh. That chance came on a visit to a cultural Centre whereby we had the opportunity through investigation and perseverance of finding and seeing a video of Ipoh. This video stirred within a feeling of a likely Centre in the future run by a Malaysian ~ but for whom? I did not know or recall at that moment of time any such person ~ Malaysian or otherwise ~ so I left it in the *ether* to show itself.

79

Singapore

On our journeys abroad our air tickets included many stopovers, some of which were Hong Kong, Singapore and Bangkok. On this journey our stopover was Singapore though we felt this was not such an important one, nevertheless, we felt to stay in Singapore to give us sufficient time to enquire if their were any Centres or peoples involved with spiritual healing or those who knew of Meditation. Of course our time was limited so the extent of our searching was confined to a small area.

The heat in Singapore was extreme, the city had excellent restaurants and shops and everywhere was exceptionally clean.

Soon it was time to leave for Australia. On arrival Linda and her partner were there to meet us and take us to the Paddington Centre.

80

Progress

*T*HOUGH Linda had already moved their furniture into the Centre there was still much to do. Furniture and linen and suchlike to be bought. More tuition with Linda regarding accounts and general running. We also had courses to take, talks to give, meetings with interested parties to organise and an exhibition to be planned for ∼ a forthcoming event called Mind, Body and Spirit. Here we intended to have a large stand to include Natural Spiritual Healing with myself promoting and answering questions on Pure Meditation.

From our talks, adverts and suchlike, patients started to come. About this time Linda's partner had a strained back, which Peter Sevananda attended to giving him a healing. He felt such relief that he became a great 'PR' person for healing and we ended up giving healing and counselling to various members of his family.

We now felt that the Paddington Centre could go forwards and that we now would move on to New Zealand ∼ once more visiting Leigh. At Leigh we once more saw devotees, gave Counselling, various talks and ended up with a Meditation Evening. The garden was full of lighted candles, it looked like fairy land all tapestried by Laugharn and Deb. It was a beautiful evening.

It felt the right time to ask Laugharn and Deb if they wanted to become a Sister Centre. We explained fully the commitment needed from them on doing this, and we asked them to give it serious thought before replying. Next day they came back with their answer ∼ "Yes please." After a few very pleasant days spent with them we packed our bags once more making our way to the South Island to explore the full potential of this beautiful island.

81

To Christchurch

ON our arrival at South Island we hired another car to help us travel as far as possible and discover as much as possible.

This journey around the Island I knew once more to be very important, not only to meet and talk with as many Kiwis as possible but also felt strongly that we were being asked to locate an ideal part of the Island to investigate a *further* Centre.

We found people in New Zealand extremely friendly, informative and very willing to assist us in any way. Wherever we went we were grateful to find motel prices were very reasonable. The restaurants served extremely good food and service and were always willing to supply dishes to suit one's taste. Wherever we happened to be, we could always find an eating house and motel. Though the journeys were long between fixed points, the roads in general were very good, the scenery grand and beautiful, so therefore our journeys never seemed that long.

In all regions and parts we found great interest in Natural Spiritual Healing and interest to a lesser degree in Pure Meditation. We met many lovely people who invited us to their homes to give talks to their friends and in some instances to give Counselling and Healing. We found this a great joy especially from the response given to our meetings and felt now, even more so, that a Centre would be received with ample support.

Having covered the major parts of the Island from Nelson down to Invercargill, we made our way to Dunedin and upwards, stopping as we felt fit until we reached Christchurch. On entering the city, which as many people know is more English than most, we immediately felt ourselves at home, and more than that an ever-deeper feeling that this could be *the* place for a Centre. Allowing this thought to rest our immediate need was to find somewhere to stay whilst contemplating our next move. On finding a motel and after a quick 'wash and brush up' we then ventured out for a walkabout around the area. We were impressed with the city in itself and of the cleanliness and facilities offered; after a while we stopped, had a quick snack, then started back to our motel.

Though not consciously seeking to find a Centre at this moment of time, on passing an Estate Agent we felt drawn to look at the many properties they had in the window. Whilst looking we were approached by a woman who we noticed was fetching something from her car. On asking us if she could be of any assistance, we replied, "No thank you." We noticed she went into the Estate Agents. As we were about to turn away she once again approached us saying, "I am sure I can help if you'd like to come in and speak with me." This was not a selling technique, so much as the words being said by a person that does not realise exactly what they are saying or how they are saying it. This happens quite often in our life and indeed it was a spiritual motivation by her - which we understood and needed to heed.

This person asked many questions about our stay here and also of our work. "Are you looking for a Centre," she asked, "Not at this present time" we replied, "Though we do feel that Christchurch would be ideal for such a place." On her asking us, "What type of place would you require if you were buying one?" we explained fully our needs also stating that we would be leaving Christchurch the following morning. "Where are you staying at present?" she asked — "at a motel room not far from here", we replied. We remained talking for a short while before taking our leave. A very nice lady, we thought, but henceforth thought no more on the subject.

The following morning we were packed ready to leave when the telephone rang. It was the lady from the Estate Agent. "I am so pleased to have caught you before you left although I am aware it is not in your mind to buy a house at present. One has just come on to the market that I feel very strongly you should see before you leave."

Why did she ring? What reason? When we had told her we were not interested in buying, this once more added up with *intuitive feel* to a loving *spiritual push*. She seemed so adamant, that and we were curious to see the full play of the *spiritual push*, we agreed. No sooner had we arrived and walked up its drive, that I turned around to Peter, saying, "This is it. We must have this house for it is to be our new Centre.' Even knowing this, I still knew that we had to go through the usual formalities of looking around the house and garden and asking about the price. We were the first people to view this property. It was a bargain. Now we had to think and act very quickly to ensure it was not sold before we had time to work out the financial situation and inform the family.

Knowing that we were leaving in a few days time for the UK, a decision had to be urgently made, no time for procrastination. As is always the case with the higher spiritual needs, we have to go in faith. This meant giving an immediate offer to ensure its' safety before completing all the complicated red tape. More often than not I have found that against all the laws of the mortal universe we have had to make decisions to buy, and make decisions against all odds which mortals would say are ridiculous — but more *spiritual souls* would say are the norm. So our answer was given in the affirmative. We were then given the name of a good solicitor who, understanding our problems, agreed to legalise the purchase of the property, and papers of which had to be signed straight away – with finalisation taking place on our return. This we knew would take several months to complete.

82

The Sister Centres

WE only had a few months at the Mother Centre in the UK before our return was needed in Australia and New Zealand.

First port of call was Australia. Our first visit was to the Paddington Centre to help tie up any loose ends businesswise, and to meet again with old and new devotees. There were talks, healings given and this is when Linda received her new name Lindama, meaning 'Loving Mother and Guide'. Many people were coming to the Centre for this very ability she had of loving and caring for all. Though the Centre was up and running and making strides, Lindama's partner was, however, becoming possessive regarding the property, and finding it very difficult to allow the staying of retreatants ~ even with regard to their using the facilities of the Centre. Though his disrespect was showing, nevertheless I must say that when he went out and about he became a very good 'PR' person for the Centre

Lindama's partner being of strong character even to the point of stubbornness made it very difficult at times for her. She, being of a gentle nature, tried to satisfy the running of the Centre alongside his demands of privacy and possession. This is never possible and unless a person is strong enough to stand up and put God first - there *will* come a breaking time within the relationship – or of one's own health. In this case it was Lindamas' health that suffered, for her partner and her own wants (or stubbornness to wisdom) came before God and Guru.

Put God first and all things will progress well, to do otherwise will cause friction and harm.

We sorted all problems out to the best of our ability, and finalising our commitments, which included reserving a large Self Realization Meditation Healing Centre stand at a 'Mind, Body and Spirit' exhibition. This was a major event to be held at Moor Park complex in a few months time, which we said we would take part in.

Now it was time to move on.

So Be It.

83

100 Highsted Road

SOUTH Island now beckoned. Our next task was to collect the keys and take possession of the house at 100 Highsted Road, Bishopdale.

On our arrival and finding all services were cut off in the house, also with full knowledge we would have to wait several weeks for the furniture to arrive, plus the fact that it was early spring and very cold with a 'blasting' wind, we felt it advisable to find a motel nearby from where we would liaise daily with the house and start buying whatever items we were in further need of for this Centre.

On the day we were informed that our furniture was to arrive, we breathed a sigh of relief, finally moving into the Centre.

Once the furniture had been placed, very easily I might say, for each piece miraculously without any thought found its own niche, we then pondered where the Meditation room would be! It was decided that the large double garage adjoined to the house would do well as a Meditation room, while our carport and further single garage could be turned into a healing and waiting room.

To cut a long story short, we did just this, aided and abetted by Ray, a devotee who took on the main work of converting the Meditation room (for which we are eternally grateful) leaving builders to finish the remainder. Of course there was much more to do as the house and grounds with its swimming pool needed attention. Enjoying all these 'doings', one of my favourite jobs was cleaning the pool of leaves and debris and seeing the change in it from dirty to sparkling blue and appealingly clean.

The beautiful trees and shrubs at this Centre are very majestic.

It has a peace and serenity about it that made one feel the presence of the Infinite Beloved.

Peter Sevananda and myself would love to sit under a fully blossomed cherry tree, shading us from the hot sun to discuss and organize our day's work. There were so many flowering blooms and many species of birds visiting the garden that sometimes we just sat and imbibed – perhaps for longer than we should have done. Though I do believe each day should be enjoyed to its fullest state.

84

Exhibition

EXHIBITION time was upon us and our journey back to Paddington, Australia to take part and set up the two stands with Lindama. It was very important for us to have room for a healing couch, some space to exhibit, and also room for people to come to me with questions on Pure Meditation. This was a four day exhibition, we were able to get a good position, so we expected to be fairly busy, as we had many helpers who volunteered and without whom we would have found it very difficult to manage. The exhibition went very well and brought many patients to the Centre and people for future courses. We were well aware of all the work that had been done over the past few days and now were very pleased to be able to go home and put our feet up.

I do feel that talks and exhibitions are so important, for they give ample opportunity to further truth and knowledge not only of the Paddington Centre but also of deeper issues affecting the whole world, this does, as we found, bring searching souls, who, then will take these truths into life – their families, thereby creating small spiritual families and outlets for others to see and follow if they so wish.

'From little acorns big trees (things) grow'

Though we had time to look around Sydney, there were but a few days left before our departure back to Christchurch.

85

A Centre Head

ON our return to Christchurch we were pleased to find enquiries awaiting us from our advertising.

Now the Centre was a little more established it felt time to put our mind to finding a suitable person, who must be of New Zealand nationality, to run this Centre. Intuitively we felt to visit the North Island where there are many devotees. Having got this far with our decision-making, it was left in the Divine hands for our guidance.

On returning to Leigh we were warmly welcomed and settled down to any work that was needed there. One afternoon we had an invitation to visit Sybil in her treetop house. Sybil was a Meditator and Healer whom we had met on previous occasions. Hearing of a 'treetop house' I wondered if we should take any climbing gear or safety net! On arrival we found the access easy to a cosy dwelling set amongst trees with Sybil awaiting our arrival. After a delicious tea we brought ourselves up to date with the latest news and then proceeded to spiritual matters.

I knew before I had been with Sybil very long that she was the one to run the Christchurch Centre; with this realization we broached the subject of Christchurch speaking of our need to return to the UK shortly, and also the need for someone to take over the Centre. 'Would you be the one?' I asked her. This took her by surprise and although she seemed delighted, she said she would like to think about it. This we agreed was necessary for her to do, it being an important step for her to take. Within a few days, with her visit to us came her answer, "Yes." I said that we were returning to Christchurch, and that on her arrival there we would need to be with her for six weeks before it necessitated us returning to the UK.

Due to Sybil's past experiences in life she was able to absorb everything that was taught and shown to her very quickly. Though much work had to be done it was a pleasurable time. Now we felt confident that the Christchurch Centre was in loving and capable hands and would go forward in helping many souls in need.

Before we left we held many Pure Meditation evenings and celebrations of many kinds. One was of the descending of Sybil's spiritual name Mananda, meaning *Mother in Bliss*.

We left for the UK taking with us many happy memories.

You may wonder how I can be so sure of the 'rightness' of so many people, buying of Centres, when and what to do at any given time. Well! this is not difficult if you keep yourself to your high intuition. Practice makes you perfect, so you learn *always* to be attuned to this *state* whereby each act will be correct for *that* moment of time ~ then its up to the *powers* that be.

Do remember never to look for the *outcome* of such actions, just go on your high intuition, and the 'fruits' will be many for everyone.

86

Malaysia - Ipoh

ON our return to England, while speaking to the family of our travels, it was brought to mind that there was a devotee from Ipoh in Malaysia now married to an Englishman who might be interested in opening up their own Centre in Ipoh.

Knowing of the need for Ipoh to have a Centre we spoke to the couple of that area's need for more spiritual knowledge. Having received a fairly uninterested response we left the matter concerned feeling not to pursue it any further with them. It had to be their decision only – for it was a big step to take and should only be taken if a marriage is secure and both are positive people with faith, devotion and determination, which, of course we told them.

It was quite a long period of time before we saw them again, when, to our surprise they asked if the offer of going to Ipoh was still open to them, and yes, they would like to go. They did.

Unfortunately their marriage, their faith, positivity and determination were not strong enough, and though we did all we could for them, including meeting them to help them forward, they eventually gave up.

They stayed with us on their return to the UK where they were welcomed with open arms full of love from all of us, and then went on their way.

Though Ipoh still lacks a Centre at the time of writing, it will have one sometime in the future, when someone else will be given the chance – for *it will happen one day.*

Many are given a chance,

Fewer take the chance,

And less still have the faith to make a
go of that chance.

87

Cornwall

CORNWALL lies in the South West of England. It is of a rugged nature being a peninsula facing the Atlantic ocean and the English Channel. It has sometimes-turbulent seas along the craggy coastline with numerous coastal walks and its inland green pastures drew us into the county whenever we had the opportunity of resting.

During one of our recent visits, when driving through the countryside, I had a very strong impression that it would not be long before we had a Centre in Cornwall. This feeling became stronger within me, eventually, I mentioned it to Peter Sevananda, saying that I felt we should start looking around at various properties in the papers and estate agents windows, whereon Peter's reply was, "In that case I feel I know the location that we need to look in." We headed in this direction and whilst Peter Sevananda was driving I attuned myself to find out more information. Going into a Meditative State, I received all I needed to know, and it was shown to me that this intuitive feeling for seeking a residence in Cornwall was important to follow up on straight away.

The same scenario that happened when in Christchurch was showing itself again.

On entering the town we knew that this *was* the right location.

On a visit to the estate agent, after explaining what we were looking for, the agent went silent for a few moments, then quietly with a smile on his face brought out a dwelling which only at that moment had come upon the market. 'I do recommend you see it' he said, and our reply was "Yes please, can we see it now?"

Once again as soon as we saw the property we both knew it to be the one for us.

During the car drive when I had gone into a Meditative State it was shown to me that this property was going to be a place whereby I would have to withdraw, now allowing the Alpha-Omega family to further practise all that they have been taught, also it was to be a place where I would do more *inner work*, more writings for publication and much more of which at this present time I am not allowed to reveal.

This would only come about if Peter Sevananda could take over full responsibility and backup in all that is needed. This I knew he would do without a second thought, for his thoughts are like mine ~ to do God's work, in any way that is needed, alongside any of his Healing and Counselling. Thus saying, and going on faith once more, knowing that we had to set things in motion before leaving Cornwall, we made negotiation for the buying of the property.

All proceeded well to the end.

The last intuitive feeling I had on completion of this property was that our faith had been rewarded, and this Centre has come into being as a 'Cave of Silence' for the depth of work that now had to be done.

So Be It.

Like all our dealing in purchsing properties, the money was never to hand and could easily not have come about ~ but it did ~ at the last moment. So we had at all times to *go in faith*.

88

Updates

SINCE the first edition of Come was published, Leigh Centre has been sold, it had fulfilled its purpose. This does not mean that there will not be another Sister Centre in the North Island - it could happen in the future if there is a need - it is in God's hands, so be it.

Many opportunities are opening up for devoted souls to take God's work forward, the opportunities are there to do so. Though none should entertain such a wonderful adventure unless they are of devotion and full faith in God and Guru enabling them to *listen* and *act* upon words of wisdom

89

The Paddington Centre

OUR Centre in Paddington Australia had to be kept for as long as people needed the experience of running it, and until there were sufficient devotees to receive and take Pure Meditation and Healing to those who are desirous of more spiritual knowledge. Yes, I know when it is time for these events to take place. It is important for a Centre or event to run its course by acting on the intuitive will of God at the *right time*, in the *right place*. In doing this I know that everything that happens will work out for the best, for every individual soul, everywhere, in every way.

This is not always easy for everybody to understand but it is completely and utterly true. I have found this to be so throughout my years of living on this earth plane.

Lindama has now passed from this earth plane. Valerie, Jim and their daughters took over the running of the Centre for a time. We had many helpers, Rosie and Janet to name but a few ~ bless them all for the work that they did for the Centre.

It was while on one of our visits to the Centre that Rosie suggested making a video of our work and the devotees. This was our first video of the Centre to be made, and we believe helps a great deal to forward the truth of Pure Meditation, Healing and Spiritual Knowledge.

90

Overseas developments

WE now have a sister Centre in Canada which is lovingly run by Alexandria and Mark, and is progressing well.

Michigan has asked that they may become a contact or Sister Centre, they have had to wait for this to happen; now is the right time and we welcome them with open arms. This Centre is run by Betty, Jenny and Scott, and it is in an area where it needs to be, for souls to come and imbibe, and gain knowledge of how to find peace love and joy in this lifetime.

Auckland in New Zealand (North Island) now has a Self Realization Meditation Healing Centre.

My dream of a Centre in this area of New Zealand has now been realized, particularly as it has a Maori and Pakaha connection which will lead to the giving and receiving from both sides which do have so much to give to each other.

Sonya Hardcastle whom we have known and trained – is fully qualified and with a heart full of love for all – is wanting only to serve God, Guru and all of its creatures great and small.

I know that she will do this, and is having the full co-operation of her family in all matters. How fortunate to have such a family.

So we welcome Sonya with this new Centre, knowing that it will provide a source of comfort for many.

Our good friends Dee and Bill who have helped us so much in the past are now residing in Spain where they are still helping people and taking in the stray animals that are found on some of Spain's beaches. We have visited them on several occasions and on their instigation they have taken courses and given talks. These were very progressive and led to more people's awareness of the spiritual truths. Bill and Dee both have the power of healing that is appreciated by many.

Harold and Joyce Pratt who bought and gifted the Mother Centre property have now passed into the light and I am sure they are continuing to help people wherever they may be. They still are much loved and missed by us all. I lovingly remember how Joyce, who loved the garden, would keep us well informed of all our 'weeds'. This was a great help to us. God bless her.

91

UK Mother Centre

THE Mother Centre has gone from strength to strength, with its courses being taken worldwide, and talks being given by members of the Alpha-Omega family in all areas ~ the breadth of the United Kingdom and in fact the world.

There are many more ways we have found for Pure Meditation and other activities to be taken out into the world. We have the Arms of the Family whereby people are invited to stay overnight and imbibe.

Worldwide there are evenings of Meditation held, and the SRMHC Lightworkers whose role it is to spread the truth, love and light of God~Guru. It would be impossible to count the many helpers/devotees of God, but what I do know is that we are eternally grateful to all of them.

The Centre must go forward ~ otherwise it goes backwards, nothing is ever static, so we have gone forward with expansion on all levels. Our latest additions are a further chalet, extra toilet facilities, as some of you know we have a further garden and pond with an Eastern theme, called the 'Garden of Serenity.'

Our next project is a much needed extra large room for Yoga and teaching, this runs alongside making a permanent base and cover for our existing swimming pool whose cover is in dire need of restoration.

There are many qualified souls who have taken our courses and are now ready to help others. Some of these people have asked to be affiliates or contacts of the Centre, others have their own family units who keep in regular touch to keep updated and receive a 'spiritual energy boost'.

Our editorial department has gone from strength to strength with the books, tapes, videos and CDs. The Self Realization Meditation Healing Centres' magazine 'Dharma's readership has grown considerably.

Slowly but surely our land and property is being returned to us.

Our land used to consist of Owl Cottage, the Lodge and the Daoseva buildings including all their grounds, plus one other cottage and land. We have regained all but one area back which one day will make up a part of the whole.

These happennings of our land and property being returned to us were told of, to me, when we first moved to Queen Camel, by one of the Masters. I never doubted that it would come to pass – but how – I did not know.

How all this came about is a miraculous story in itself, but not one to be told here.

The message that I received from my Guru, Paramahansa Yogananda is now coming into fruition. He asked that small families should take Pure Meditation into their lives, that individuals should *live* Pure Meditation in their hearts, with meeting places for like-minded souls.

We need to remember that bricks and mortar do not house God, that it is *each person* with their light shining brightly that goes amongst the many ~ that will save themselves and the world.

The Alpha-Omega family changes and grows as intended by the powers that be.

The Truth Eternal

why it was written

I am not a writer – as such. After writing the first edition of 'Come' my first feelings were of relief, knowing I had done what had been needed of me and joy that it had ben completed.

No more books said I.

Yet there were more to come, with Truth Eternal being my last.

Truth Eternal was written after being told in no uncertain terms that Gods devotees needed more truths — more knowledge, and, that I needed to write a further book for them. This person was speaking from a very deep spiritual level, not of themselves entirely.

I then realized the importance of what was being said — and needed. My thanks

and

Gods will be done
at
all times.

Notes

1 Royal Air Force
2 British Overseas Airways Corporation.
3 Give them brown tones rather than black.
4 Overdrawn at the Bank.
5 *Au pair* – One who looks after children.
6 Seats up near the ceiling.
7 In those days buses ran most of the night and there was a depot near us.
8 Do It Yourself or Self–build.
9 Diploma of Remedial Electrolysis.
10 Value Added Tax.
11 Spiritual Association of Great Britain.
12 Lotus petals of the chakras — as they open we perceive more.
13 Abbreviation for a Tibetan monks name.
14 S.R.F. — The Self–Realization Fellowship started by Guruji and built up into a large spiritual organization; many moons ago in California, USA.
15 ji — in India is a respectful suffix.
16 Paramahansa means white swan — highest.
17 Mahasaya, loosely translated, means *breadth and width in vision and thought.*
18 "My Father and I are one." There is no separation, only that which we make in our own minds.
19 A well known magician.
20 The Higher Self is the embodiment wherein dwells the Christ Power, God's wisdom.
21 Tracey was her baptised name, later she became known as Rowena Dharma.
22 Transcendental Meditation

This Centre is a house of direction, with many paths to choose from — but only one true path in accordance with *GOD's* wishes.

To all who take this path it will have its difficulties, but the rewards are great — true peace and happiness, if you desire these, then you will need a hand to guide you.

It is *HERE ~ STAY* and be helped first, towards *SELF–REALIZATION* and then all your needs will be met.

Beliefs and Aims of the Centre

1. The spreading of the truth.
2. That there is no death, only organised life.
3. That scientific and spiritual knowledge lead to Self~Realization, peace and harmony.
4. To bring harmony to the mind, body and spirit of all God's living creatures.
5. To show that *LOVE* is the strongest energy force that there is, anywhere.
6. To show that all people and all religions will lead eventually to the one and same pathway, to Self~Realization and God.
7. That knowledge will dispel ignorance and fear and make us whole.
8. To provide pure thoughts to beget high minds.
9. To find our true selves through Pure Meditation.
10. To rid ourselves of all negative states of the mind and body.
11. To spread unconditional love throughout the world.
12. To uphold the wisdom of the Masters, such as Ji Jesus, Babaji, Buddha and the Saints.
13. To prove that there are many Masters and many Mansions ~ for us all.

BUT ONLY ONE GOD.

Meditation
is
The Way

The Self Realization
Meditation Healing Centre

The Self Realization Meditation Healing Centre was founded in the Ether, then in the heart of Mata Yogananda. The Centre's given emblem of the 'I am' is shown on all the Self Realization Meditation Healing Centre material ~ so that people may know that they are dealing authentically with the Centre.

For information on Pure Meditation, Natural Spiritual Healing, Progressive Counselling and other courses, please contact:

Self Realization Meditation Healing Centre
Laurel Lane, Queen Camel, Yeovil, Somerset, BA22 7NU, UK.
Tel. 01935 850266   Fax. 01935 850234

Internet: http://www.selfrealizationcentres.org
E-mail: info@selfrealizationcentres.org

Sister Centres:

18 Cunliffe Place, Glenfield, Auckland,
New Zealand.
Ph./Fax. 09 441 9446

100 Highsted Road, Bishopdale,
Christchurch, **New Zealand.**
Ph. 03 359 8507   Fax. 03 359 3430

8904 Armstrong Way, Halfmoon Bay,
B.C. VON 1Y2, **Canada.**
Tel. & Fax. (604) 740 0898

7187 Drumheller Road, Bath,
MI 48808, **USA.**
Ph. (517) 641–6201 Fax. (517) 641 8336

Contact Centres:

Australia, Blue Mountains:
Tel/Fax. 02 4756 2042
Mobile 0415 543473

Switzerland, Langenthal:
Tel. 062 922 8187 Fax. 062 922 8127

New Zealand, Nelson:
Ph./Fax. (03) 540 3970

New Zealand, Masterton:
Ph./Fax. (06) 378 0990

INDEX

✺ Light Up The World! ✺
Meditation Evenings Worldwide

*to bring souls together to imbibe
and go forward to Self–Realization*

It was with great joy that the first Open Meditation evening was held at the Mother Centre many years ago; souls coming together to imbibe Divine Peace and Love, to seek Self–Realization through Pure Meditation. Since that time many Open Meditation evenings have come into being around the world ~ like stars of Love shining their light into the darkness of separation, delusion and suffering.

We hope that many more souls will be moved to open their hearts and their homes in this way, until the world is full of the Light it so urgently needs.

We look forward to you joining us ~ in the list that follows you will find your nearest Meditation Evening. Please ring for details.

These Meditation Evenings, and the Arms of the Family, are expanding all the time ~ please contact the UK Mother Centre for further details and contacts.

The peace~oneness in Meditation ~ joy for all to share.

Meditation Evenings Worldwide

UK Mother Centre

Somerset, Queen Camel ✦ Monday - Saturday 8.45 for 9pm Meditation, Sundays 7.45 for 8pm Meditation ✦ (01935) 850266

UK

Bath, Bathford ✦ Thursdays weekly, 8.30pm for 8.45pm Meditation
Wendy Allen ✦ (01225) 852550
Bristol, Pensford ✦ Mondays 8.30pm weekly
Julia Raffo and Michael Simmons ✦ (01761) 490556
Bristol, St. Andrews ✦ 8.30pm last Tuesday of each month
Lindy Gibbon ✦ (0117) 944 2711
Devon, Newton Abbott ✦ 7.45pm for 8pm Meditation, first Sunday of each month ✦ Rowena Dharma Nicholson and Jason Hinrich ✦ (01803 872041)
Devon, South Molton ✦ 6.30 for 7pm Meditation, first Thursday of each month ✦ Sarah Beanland ✦ (01598) 760592
Hampshire, Alton ✦ 7.45 for 8pm Meditation, first Monday of each month
Melanie Pickard ✦ (01420) 549886
London, N19 ✦ from 6pm, first Sunday of each month
Deborah Munnelly ✦ (0207) 700 6557
Scotland, Edinburgh ✦ Saturdays, weekly, 8.45 for 9pm Meditation
Satay Singh ✦ (0131) 467 0828/Mobile 07811 853319
Somerset, Frome ✦ Wednesdays 8.30pm weekly and other times by request
Charles Kemp and Sara Crowley ✦ (01373) 462606
Somerset, Glastonbury ✦ Wednesdays, weekly 7.45 for 8pm Meditation
Carol and Terry Palmer ✦ (01458) 831353
Somerset, Martock ✦ Tuedays weekly, 8.45 for 9pm Meditation
Rossananda and Mahseeman Seva Young ✦ (01935) 824142
Somerset, Wells ✦ Tuesdays weekly, 7.45 for 8pm Meditation
Joy Buchanan ✦ (01934) 712082 ✦ Caroline Bruce ✦ (01749) 870873
Wales, Brecon ✦ 7.30 for 8pm Meditation, first Monday of each month
Fee & Richard Curtis ✦ (01874) 624067
Yorkshire, Richmond ✦ 8.30pm first Wednesday of each month
Maureen Clayton ✦ 01748 886188

Australia

Blue Mountains, Mount Wilson, ✦ Sundays 7.30pm weekly
Suzzane and Denis Daly ✦ 024756 2042/Mobile 0415 543473

Meditation Evenings Worldwide

Canada

British Columbia, Halfmoon Bay ✦ Monday-Saturday 8.45 for 9pm
Meditation, Sundays 7.45 for 8pm Meditation
Canadian SRMHC Centre (604) 740 0898
British Columbia, North Vancouver ✦ 10.30am, third Sunday of each month
Noel Hanuse ✦ (604) 983 9661
British Columbia, Madeira Park ✦ 10.30am, last Sunday of each month,
please call ahead to confirm ✦ Carrie and Keith Shaw ✦ (604) 883 9195

Germany

Baden-Wuerttemberg, Waldkirch ✦ 8.30pm, first Sunday of each month
Renate Schölz ✦ 7681 490792

New Zealand

South Island, Christchurch ✦ Monday-Saturday 8.45 for 9pm Meditation
Sundays 7.45 for 8pm Meditation
Christchurch SRMHC Centre ✦ (03) 359 8507
North Island, Auckland ✦ Sundays 7.30 for 7.45pm Meditation
Auckland SRMHC Centre ✦ (09) 441 9446
South Island, Nelson ✦ Sundays 7.45pm weekly
Paul and Victoria Woodward ✦ (03) 540 3970
North Island, Auckland ✦ Wednesdays 8.15 for 8.30pm first, third and fifth
Wednesday of each month ✦ Adriana Tuscia ✦ (09) 360 8616
North Island, Auckland ✦ Tuesdays 8.30pm weekly
Susan Okeby ✦ (09) 479 6368/Mobile 021 479 363
North Island, Auckland & North Shore ✦ Wednesdays 8.15 for 8.30pm
second and fourth Wednesday of each month
Margaret Tabuteau ✦ (09) 445 3657
North Island, Warkworth (Matakana) ✦ Sundays 7.45 for 8pm first & third
Sunday of each month ✦ Colette Taylor ✦ (09) 422 5255
North Island, Masterton ✦ Sundays 7.45 for 8pm
Ràna Webster and Dev Verma ✦ (06) 378 0990

Switzerland

Switzerland, Langenthal ✦ Wednesdays 8.30pm weekly
Franziska Fischer ✦ 062 922 8187

USA

Michigan, Lansing ✦ Monday - Saturday 8.45 for 9pm Meditation, Sundays
7.45 for 8pm Meditation ✦ Michigan SRMHC Centre ✦ (517) 641 6201

Arms of the Family

The Arms of the Family offer bed and breakfast and/or dinner to students/friends of the worldwide Self Realization Meditation Healing Centres: for those friends who are travelling and wish to find a loving place to rest their heads 'en route' and know that they will be welcome. In this way we hope to bring a sharing of life with those of a like mind.

Please ring the UK Mother Centre for further contacts and details.

UK

Bristol, Nailsea ◆ Roger Furneaux ◆ (01275) 853786
Bristol, Pensford ◆ Julia Raffo and Michael Simmons ◆ (01761) 490556
Essex, Clacton-on-Sea ◆ Geraldine and Paul Maitland-Edwards ◆ (01255) 425113
Hampshire, New Forest ◆ Mike Barker and Lorraine Stephens ◆ (02380) 814048
London, Wimbledon ◆ Jacqueline Withers ◆ (0208) 947 4859
Somerset, Martock ◆ Rossananda and Mahseeman Seva Young ◆ (01935) 824142
Somerset, Wells ◆ Joy and Alan Buchanan ◆ (01934) 712082
Somerset, Wyke Champflower (Nr. Bruton)
Noreen Daniel and Eileen Lemon ◆ (01749) 812788
Wales, Brecon ◆ Fee & Richard Curtis ◆ (01874) 624067
Wales, Brecon ◆ Gabelle and Michael Eisele ◆ (01874) 690116
Wales, Powys ◆ Mark Chappell ◆ (01686) 412307
Yorkshire, Richmond ◆ Maureen Clayton ◆ (01748) 886188

Australia

Blue Mountains, Mount Wilson ◆ Suzzane and Denis Daly
024756 2042/Mobile 0415 543473
New South Wales, Sydney ◆ Daodeva Westward ◆ 02 9896 6917

Canada

British Columbia, Madeira Park ◆ Carrie and Keith Shaw ◆ (604) 883 9195
Alberta, Edmonton ◆ Keith and Nicole Bradford ◆ (780) 450 9836/Mobile (780) 920 2495

New Zealand

South Island, Nelson ◆ Paul and Victoria Woodward ◆ (03) 540 3970
North Island, Masterton ◆ Ràna Webster and Dev Verma ◆ (06) 378 0990

Switzerland

Langenthal ◆ Franziska Fischer ◆ 062 922 8187

All the Self Realization Meditation Healing Centres are here for you.
If you need further information of any kind, please do contact us.

Help us Help Others!

Dear Reader,

The Self Realization Meditation Healing Centre is a registered charity helping and guiding all. We teach Pure Meditation, train professional healers, counsellors and teachers, and offer retreats for those in need.

Much of our work involves helping those suffering from all forms of physical and mental illness, stress, and trauma.

You can help us to help people in need.

Any donation would make an enormous difference to our voluntary work and would be gratefully received.

Your total donation will go directly to:

• Help those in need receive Natural Spiritual Healing, Progressive Counselling, Pure Meditation and any other form of therapy that they need at the Centre.
• A bursary fund to help people take our self-help courses who cannot meet their full cost.

There are many other ways to help us ~ a Tithe Box (available at the Centres) and the Sustainers Fund. *Legacies are gratefully accepted.*

If you would like to receive further information on the above or on the Centre, please contact us:

Self Realization Meditation Healing Centre
Laurel Lane, Queen Camel, Yeovil, Somerset, BA22 7NU, UK.
Tel. 01935 850266   Fax. 01935 850234

Internet: http://www.selfrealizationcentres.org
E-mail: info@selfrealizationcentres.org

*Your donation **will** make a difference*

Thank you for reading.

348

Other Publications by Mata Yogananda available from Daoseva Press

Daoseva Press

Books

Self~Realization Through Meditation *ISBN 0952273470*
The Truth Eternal ISBN 0 9522734 4 6
Poems of the Heart ISBN 0 9522734 9 7
Song~Soul Chants Music book *ISBN* 0 9522734 3 8
Song~Soul Chants ("Small songbook")
Perfect Thoughts Music book
Spiritual Families and Centres
~ an Unknown Journey ISBN 0 9522734 0 3

Videos

~ Imbibe in Mata Yogananda's wisdom ~ in person.
Centres of Light ★ Talks With Mata Yogananda
A Message from Mata ★ Questions and Answers with Mata

Videos are supplied on cassette (VHS/PAL) Some are available in the NTSC format.
Please contact your nearest Centre for details.

DHARMA *Magazine*

Dharma is the Centres' yearly magazine presenting the Wisdom of God~Life and the Masters; with articles by Mata Yogananda and people in different professional fields including those in holistic health care. The emphasis is on practical spirituality, covering all aspects of life. Please contact the Centre to order the current issue of Dharma. Subscriptions (three and five year) and back issues are also available. ISSN 1366–3550

Photographs of Mata

We are delighted to now have available photographs of Mata in a beautiful glossy finish. Yours to treasure, these photos will bring Mata's light to your whole being.

Inspiring Talk Tapes & Song ~ Chants by Mata Yogananda

In the Inspiring Talks series, Mata Yogananda talks on real life issues with love and understanding; of the difficulties we all must overcome in our progress back to consciousness of our spiritual nature. Mata has recorded these talks so that her words may reach out to those not able to be with her, but who are needing the encouragement and demonstration that it is possible to live a God–centred life in this world today.

Also available, on CD, are two collections of Mata Yogananda's Song~Chants; *Vibrations of Love* and *Perfect Thoughts*. Each contains Song~Chants given to and performed by Mata Yogananda for the upliftment of all, recorded live, in an informal way in the UK. Companion word and music booklets to each of these beautiful CDs are also available separately. Please contact us for further details.

For all authentic publications of the Self Realization Meditation Healing Centre by Daoseva Press, please contact your nearest authorised dealer or Centre for prices and availability.

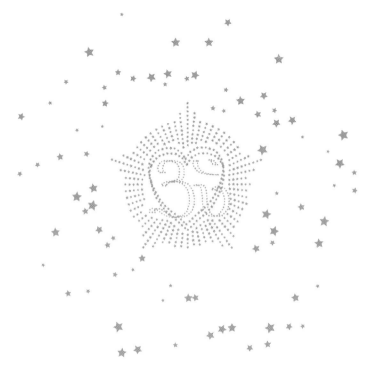

We are all stars